2019

Mindy -

You are precious

to our ___ Father

& He ___ plans

for you

Love,
Michael
Meghan
Adam

♡

PLATINUM FAITH

AKA
Aunt
Miss

MICHELLE MEDLOCK ADAMS & BETHANY JETT

PLATINUM FAITH

LIVE BRILLIANT, BE RESILIENT, & KNOW YOUR WORTH

Abingdon Press
Nashville

Dedication

MICHELLE

This book is dedicated to my late parents, Walter and Marion Medlock, the finest people I've ever known. Not only did they raise me in a Christian home and teach me about Jesus but they also lived out their faith every single day. The joy of the Lord bubbled out of them, and their steadfast faith continues to inspire me even now. This one's for you, Mom and Dad. Your legacy of faith lives on in our family.

BETHANY

This book is dedicated to my parents, Jeffery Donley and Johnnie Alexander, for teaching me the truth of Scripture and how to live daily for Jesus. I love you both so much and will always be grateful for your example.

This book is also dedicated to Steve Frazee, for the love of Bazooka-Zooka bubblegum, Stuart, and PN's. But most of all, for being the person who made me fall in love with youth ministry and for teaching me to own my faith. #1.

Contents

Contents

Foreword

Growing up working in my family's jewelry store, I quickly learned the differences among all of the precious metals—particularly platinum, white gold, and sterling silver. One of the unique characteristics of platinum is that it won't tarnish like other precious metals. While we had to polish our store's sterling silver pieces with a special cloth on a regular basis, we never had to do that to the platinum ones. Platinum always shines brilliantly. That's why when my friend Michelle Medlock Adams told me she was coauthoring a book called *Platinum Faith* I thought it made perfect sense. Because when we have faith—platinum faith—it causes us to shine brightly for Jesus.

The apostle Paul defines faith as the substance of things hoped for and the evidence of things not seen. In other words, faith is being sure that the things we hope for will come to pass and being certain that the things that we cannot see do indeed exist.

Many of us are raised in families that attend church, pray regularly, and honor God. From an early age we learn that we were created by God and that through His son, Jesus, we receive salvation and eternal life. Others come to know God in different ways, perhaps through a friend or by watching a minister on TV, or even through a traumatic life experience. Regardless of how we were introduced to God, this introduction, while an important first step, is only the beginning.

You may say, "I believe in God, and because I can't actually see Him, I have faith." That would be true because you have attained "a certainty in something you cannot see." But understand this: believing in God and His son, Jesus, is only the introduction to your faith. The true richness and fullness of your faith is only realized once you understand the relationship God desires to have with you.

If we are to live out our faith to the fullest, we must understand how important we are to God, how much He cherishes us, and how He longs to give us the requests of our hearts. The Bible says that it is God's desire that you have a hope and a future. This is the promise that gives you strength in times of adversity, determination to reach for your dreams, and the confidence that you are valuable to the Creator of the universe. This promise is why you can be sure that the things you hope for will come to pass.

When the apostle Paul defined faith in Ephesians 11:1, one thing he did not say was that having or holding your faith would be easy. In fact, he likened keeping the faith with fighting a good fight. Faith, like all things worth having, doesn't just happen. It takes diligence, work, and all the help we can get.

That is why I appreciate this book, *Platinum Faith*, by my dear friend Michelle Medlock Adams and Bethany Jett. *Platinum Faith*, as its name implies, is a blueprint on how to take your faith to the highest level. Through it, Michelle and Bethany will help you realize your value not only to God but to the world around you. Read each chapter carefully, explore the scriptures they present, and open your heart and mind to the wisdom they offer. If you do this, your spirit will be renewed, your relationship with God will grow stronger, and you will experience a faith like you have never known before.

Victoria Osteen

Copastor of Lakewood Church and
New York Times best-selling author

Preface

When Bethany and I decided to start our literary business in the spring of 2017, we prayed over every aspect of our partnership—especially the choosing of the name. It had to be just right. It had to stand out in the crowded publishing world, but also it had to reflect the two of us. After researching several names we'd been batting around, we didn't feel settled on any particular one until Bethany looked up over the top of her laptop and said, "What about Platinum Literary?"

I immediately liked it.

As we studied the various properties associated with platinum, we liked our choice even more. It's rare; it's remarkably resistant to corrosion; it's very useful; it's quite precious; and it's able to withstand the heat, to name just a few.

Fast-forward to February 2018. Bethany and I were both teaching at the Florida Christian Writers Conference at Lake Yale, and our wonderful agent, Cyle Young, set up a breakfast appointment for us to meet with an editor from a publishing house we'd been hoping to break into, but there was just one problem.

We didn't have a book to pitch.

We'd been so busy with our own individual deadlines that we hadn't had the opportunity to come up with a new book idea to pitch, yet we had this meeting scheduled. So, at 2:18 a.m. the morning of the meeting, Bethany and I were texting back and forth, trying to come up with an idea worthy of this publishing house.

I texted, "What if we do a book called 'Platinum Faith' and discuss each platinum property and how it applies to our faith?"

"Yesssss!!!!" she texted back.

So, for the next forty-five minutes, we basically outlined the book you hold in your hands today. And, let me tell you, this has been a journey of faith!

You know how people always say, "Don't pray for patience because you'll be tested in that area"? Well, we discovered that as we wrote each chapter, dealing with a different aspect of platinum faith, we were tested in that area, or sometimes, we were flat out under attack! That's how we knew this book was extra special—because the enemy has been fighting us so hard during the development and writing of every section of every chapter. From unexpected deployments to crazy teeth issues to moving houses in the final stretch to finding out a loved one has a brain tumor—it's been a season of major challenges, a few meltdowns, and intense growing pains.

We discovered these difficult days were the perfect setup to develop our platinum faith.

God knew we would have to walk this out in order to put it all on paper. We both feel like it's the most authentic, raw, and vulnerable writing we've ever done, and so we share our hearts with you—the good, the bad, and the sometimes ugly.

We are storytellers. We are writers. We are teachers and inspirational speakers. We are wives. We are moms. We are sisters and friends. We are lovers of the Word. But we are not ordained ministers. We don't have degrees in Bible, though we are students of the Word. So, we don't claim to have all the answers, but we know the One who does.

We invite you to dig into the Word of God with us. We hope you'll dog-ear pages and highlight passages and share powerful quotes with your friends and family. But more than anything, we pray that our book calls you into a deeper relationship with Jesus and prods you down the path to platinum faith.

Know that you've been prayed over as we wrote this book, and that we truly believe you picked up *Platinum Faith* by divine appointment.

If there was ever a time in history that we needed to be filled up and ready to walk in our callings, it's now. So, what do you say, sister? Are you ready to take this journey of faith with us?

Let the platinum process begin.

INTRODUCTION

The Platinum Process

Scripture says that to each of us is given a measure of faith (see Romans 12:3). How we apply that faith is up to each one of us. That's why this book is so important. We want to become more Christlike and grow in our faith so that we can live brilliant in our calling, be resilient when the enemy's attacks come, and truly know our worth.

The Bible says to keep our eyes on Jesus, the Author and Perfecter of our faith (Hebrews 12:2). It's our belief that understanding how the properties of this precious metal compare with who God created us to be can lead to a strong, unshakeable, platinum faith.

In chapters 2 through 13 there are four sections of which to take note:

PLATINUM PROPERTY

Here's where we dip our toes into science class. The Platinum Property sections include an explanation of a specific characteristic of platinum and compare that property to how we can grow in our faith.

PLATINUM PROMISE

God's Word is the source of all truth. In the Platinum Promise section, we'll explore biblical examples of ordinary people living out their faith in extraordinary ways and identify how we can learn from them.

LIVE BRILLIANT

We took turns writing each chapter so the Live Brilliant section brings in the other author's voice, thoughts, and perspective on how to merge the properties and the promises of having a platinum faith.

PLATINUM PROJECT

Rounding out each chapter is the Platinum Project where we offer a takeaway, application, or encouragement so that you can own this aspect of platinum faith and make it your own.

OUR PLATINUM PRAYER FOR YOU

You are a woman of faith.
A woman of grace.
A woman of God's strength.
It is our prayer that the words in this book are used to edify, encourage, empower, and most of all, help you stretch and shine for Him in ways you may never have thought of before. What we found as we wrote these chapters was that there were so many areas that we needed to grow ourselves. God used this book to show us how we can continue to learn and be used for Him.

It's our prayer that you have a similar experience and we'd love to connect with you and hear about it.

We're in this together, we women of platinum faith.

. . . and here we go!

CHAPTER 1

All-in Faith

MICHELLE

Living a life of faith means never knowing where you are being led—but it does mean loving and knowing the One who is leading. It is literally a life of FAITH, not of understanding and reason—a life of knowing Him who calls us to go.

Oswald Chambers

It was a beautiful day on Lake Okeechobee. The bass were biting. The weather was near perfect. And, I was getting to spend some quality time with my husband, Jeff. We had traveled to Florida, hoping for a little rest and relaxation before his tax season began and my looming book deadlines descended, but all of that changed with one phone call.

"What's wrong, Ab?" I asked, trying to understand our oldest daughter between her sobs. "Is it one of the kids?"

We knew Abby had taken our eighteen-month-old grandson, Bear, to the pediatrician earlier in the day for what she suspected was an ear infection, but we figured the doctor would prescribe some antibiotics and that would be that.

"I'm on my way to the hospital to meet with a pediatric neurologist. They think Bear may have a brain tumor."

As I tried to comprehend what she was saying, I did my best to keep it together. I needed to be a strong mama for Abby so she could be a strong mama for Bear.

The next few hours seemed like days. I felt helpless. We were in the middle of the lake, waiting on news from Abby. I was already on my phone, trying to get a flight out of Fort Myers for that night, when I saw Abby's number pop up.

"Mom," Ab said, her voice cracking. "It's not good."

I took a deep breath.

"They found a tumor on Bear's brainstem. That's all we know right now. I'll call you after we meet with the whole team of doctors. Are you coming?"

"Yes, I'm trying to get a flight out now," I answered. "Ab, I just can't believe this."

As she continued explaining what the MRI had shown, I stood frozen, looking up into the beautiful blue sky, silently praying.

And just like that, a small rainbow appeared out of nowhere. It hadn't been raining. It wasn't cloudy. In fact, it was really sunny that afternoon. Yet, there it was—a beautiful rainbow—Bear's size.

"Abby, you'll never believe what I'm looking at right now! God just put a rainbow in the sky! As you were telling me about the MRI results, the rainbow appeared out of nowhere! I truly believe that's a sign from God. He's got this!"

I snapped a picture with my phone so I'd always remember that moment, and I sent it to Abby so she could have it, too.

As I write this chapter, we're only weeks out from Bear's original diagnosis, and we await the next MRI to see if the tumor is aggressive, to see if it's cancerous, to see what treatment options are available. But as we wait, we pray. We pray all the time. And, thousands join us in prayer.

I don't know how this story will end. I know how I'd like it to end. I'm believing that God will simply obliterate that tumor on Bear's brainstem as only Jehovah Rapha, the Lord our Healer, can. I'm believing when they do another MRI, the neurologist won't be able to find that tumor. It'll simply be gone. That's my hope. And, when that miracle transpires, I will shout the testimony all over the world.

But, if God chooses to handle this situation another way, I'm still going to trust Him. I'm still going to love Him. And, I'm still going to serve Him. I'm all in. That's the only way I want to live.

How about you? Are you living that all-in kind of faith? If you have ever experienced any miracles in your life, then you can't help but have that all-in kind of faith. We've experienced a few miracles in our own family. We know God is able. But I also know that God doesn't always do things the way I think He should, and there have been times in my life when I didn't understand why He didn't intervene. I bet you've had those times, too. During those seasons, you have to dig your heels in and stand strong in your faith. You don't have to understand God to have faith in Him. The Bible tells us that His ways are higher than our ways, right (Isaiah 55:8-9)?

On the days when my faith isn't exactly platinum, I think about that rainbow, and I praise God for His promises. I remind myself that God is bigger than my greatest fears, and I begin to feed my spirit with the Word of God.

PURSUING PLATINUM FAITH

That's how we pursue platinum faith. By building up our spirit with God's Word. And, by getting to know Him—not just knowing *about* Him but really getting to know Who He is.

Because if you know Him through His Word and meditate on His more than seven thousand promises, you'll begin to experience His goodness and faithfulness, and you'll trust Him—no matter what. You'll know that God, your Abba Father, has a plan for your life (Jeremiah 29:11) and that He has solutions for problems you haven't yet encountered. You'll know that when a crisis arises—like it has with my sweet grandson's health—that God wasn't surprised by it. You'll be able to rest in Him, knowing He is aware, on call, and working on your behalf.

But, the only way to know Him so intimately is to spend time with Him. In His Word. In His House. In prayer. Listening to praise and worship music and Christian podcasts. Watching Christian broadcasts. Immersing yourself in Him. That's how you pursue platinum faith on purpose.

We need to eat of God's Word every single day. Last year I researched dinosaurs for a children's book I was writing, and I was astounded to learn the T. rex only ate about once a week. I bet that was one massive meal, don't you? But we are not like T. rex.

We need daily nourishment in the Word. That's why it's called "our daily bread." Ever heard the expression, "You can't live on yesterday's manna"? It's true.

So, dig in every day! Eat up! Get to know God. Press into His promises. Proclaim His goodness no matter your circumstances! You see, platinum faith isn't moved or shaken by the situation. Platinum faith looks the negative situation right in the eyeballs and says, "But God!" Platinum faith is that all-in kind of faith—the kind of faith that isn't moved by the circumstances or even by the outcome.

That's the kind of faith the woman with the issue of blood had in Mark 5. Remember that story? Let's read it together:

> *A large crowd followed and pressed around him. And a woman was there who had been subject to bleeding for twelve years. She had suffered a great deal under the care of many doctors and had spent all she had, yet instead of getting better she grew worse. When she heard about Jesus, she came up behind him in the crowd and touched his cloak, because she thought, "If I just touch his clothes, I will be healed." Immediately her bleeding stopped and she felt in her body that she was freed from her suffering.*
>
> *At once Jesus realized that power had gone out from him. He turned around in the crowd and asked, "Who touched my clothes?"*
>
> *"You see the people crowding against you," his disciples answered, "and yet you can ask, 'Who touched me?'"*
>
> *But Jesus kept looking around to see who had done it. Then the woman, knowing what had happened to her, came and fell at his feet and, trembling with fear, told him the whole truth. He said to her, "Daughter, your faith has healed you. Go in peace and be freed from your suffering"* (Mark 5:24-34 NIV).

Not only was this woman chronically ill, which meant she was probably very weak so pushing through the crowd was no doubt physically challenging, but also this bleeding condition made her ceremonially unclean according to Jewish law (Leviticus 15:25-27). In her condition, she shouldn't have been in the temple at all, and she certainly shouldn't have been bumping up against people in the crowd. In fact, according to the Law, anyone or anything she touched would've been deemed unclean. But she didn't care. She knew Jesus was in her midst, and she believed He could heal her if she could only get to Him.

She'd already tried everything else. She'd spent all of her money on doctors and medicine, yet she was still sick. She was out of options . . . but God.

She risked it all when she reached for His cloak.

Just when she thought she'd gotten away with it, Jesus stops and asks, "Who touched my robe?" In reality, dozens of people were touching his robe. After all, He was in the middle of a large crowd so the disciples thought his question was a silly one, but she didn't. She knew she'd been found out, so she courageously comes forward, falls at the feet of Jesus, and tells Him everything. But Jesus doesn't condemn her. Instead, He rewards her faith and says, "Daughter, your faith has healed you. Go in peace and be freed from your suffering."

Have you ever been so desperate for a touch from Jesus that you were willing to risk it all? I know it's scary to step outside of your comfort zone, but let me encourage you to "do it afraid." You see, faith isn't the absence of fear; but rather, faith is being courageous enough to step out when you don't know what will happen, when the odds are stacked against you, when it's safer to stay right where you are. That's what the woman with the issue of blood did, and she received her miracle that day.

The Bible doesn't tell us this, but I believe she was probably saying in a hushed voice, "If I just touch His cloak, I'll be healed," over and over again. As she made her way to the temple. As she pushed through the crowd. And, as she took that one big leap of faith and reached out to touch Jesus.

Because the Bible says that faith comes by hearing and hearing by the Word of God (Romans 10:17), I often say scriptures out loud and make powerful Word-based declarations when I'm going through something. I need to hear myself saying those faith-filled words, and it's like I'm putting the enemy on notice that I trust in God and His promises. Then, I'll recall all of the times God has come through for me and for my loved ones, and I'll praise Him for His faithfulness in each and every situation. (I call that getting my "sassy faith" on.)

PLATINUM PROMISE

This is a biblical principle. That's exactly what David did before he faced the mighty giant Goliath (1 Samuel 17). You see, David already had a track record of victory. The scriptures tell us he had already defeated the lion and the bear while taking care of his father's sheep. So when he came up against the giant, David had no doubt he would defeat him, too. Others looked at the giant and said, "He is too big to kill," but David looked at Goliath and said, "That giant is too big to miss!"

It works the same way in our daily lives. Rehearse those past victories and stand strong as you wait for that next breakthrough, that next answer, that next miracle. Praise God for those breakthroughs, answers, and miracles before you ever see them.

Hebrews 11:1 says, "Now faith is the substance of things hoped for, the evidence of things not seen" (NKJV).

The world says, "I'll believe it when I see it." Faith says, "I'll believe it even though I can't see it, and then I will see it come to pass."

That's easy to say, but not as easy to live. My longtime friends Clay and Tina Caldwell are shining examples of really standing on the Word of God and believing against all odds. They had to have that fearless kind of faith—platinum faith—to see their miracle manifest.

In her twentieth week of pregnancy, Tina went in for another ultrasound, hoping for a good report, but something was wrong. She knew it.

Tina lay on the cold table, sobbing, while her sister stood nearby praying silently.

A few minutes later, a specialist came in.

"Tina," he said, "your water has broken, but it's much too early for the baby to be born."

Tina felt numb all over. When her husband, Clay, arrived, the doctor explained the facts and offered two options: take the baby immediately or wait for Tina to go into natural labor. Either way, he told them that the baby had little chance for survival.

"We believe in miracles," Clay said. "Let's wait and give God a chance to work."

Tina and Clay went home and prayed for a miracle. Three weeks later, Tina's body went into natural labor. They rushed to the hospital and discovered that Tina's cervix had begun dilating.

A specialist in high-risk deliveries was called in to examine her. After studying her ultrasound, he leaned back in his chair but said nothing. A few moments later, the doctor turned off the machine.

"I'm sorry," he said. "I can't offer you any hope that your baby will survive being born this early."

The doctor left the room, but the finality of his words hung in the air.

Clay held Tina's hand as the doctor delivered their tiny baby—it was a girl!

Tina instinctively shouted, "God, please breathe the breath of life in her!" At that moment, Clay decided the baby's name would be Zoë, which means "life."

Clay had been told the baby would be small, but he was not prepared for what he saw. She was purple. Her ears were only half-formed. Her legs were drawn up, and her skin was transparent—so thin her veins and organs were visible.

Baby Zoë weighed only 1 pound, 3.5 ounces and was 8 inches long.

She had a 1 percent chance of survival.

After Tina was stabilized, Clay staggered into the hospital hallway and fell to his knees. Several nurses cried alongside him. Later that day, Zoë lay under a heat lamp. Her head was covered with a tiny pink hat. She was so small, that Clay's wedding ring fit over her arm. Tubes and monitors surrounded the little life, but so did the glory of God.

Clay copied scriptures and taped them to Zoë's incubator. Philippians 1:6 became their promise: "And I am convinced and sure of this very thing, that He Who began a good work in you will continue until the day of Jesus Christ [right up to the time of His return], developing [that good work] and perfecting and bringing it to full completion in you" (AMPC).

During Zoë's first three months of life, she overcame tremendous medical hurdles.

"Her health changed every fifteen minutes," Clay remembered. "It was a real struggle to not give in to your emotions."

Against all odds, Zoë thrived. The doctors and nurses could offer no medical explanations, but Tina and Clay knew the reason—God, the Great Physician, had taken over and was caring for their daughter.

Weighing 4 pounds, 3 ounces, Zoë was released from the hospital on June 3, 1997. And, today, more than twenty years later, Zoë is a happy, healthy, living testimony of God's faithfulness. Clay, Tina, and Zoë share their testimony every chance they get, hoping to encourage others to stand on the Word of God and not be moved by the circumstances.

Live Brilliant:
The Healing Edges

BETHANY

It's important to understand why the woman who was bleeding specifically touched the edge of Jesus's garment. In Greek the word is *kraspedon* and "can also refer to the tassel that the Israelites wore on the four corners of the cloak."[1]

The *tzitzit* are the fringes of the prayer shawls that God instructs the Israelites to attach to their garments to be physical reminders of the commandments of God (see Number 15:37-41). Malachi 4:2 says, "The sun of righteousness shall rise with healing in its wings" (ESV). Some have interpreted this passage to mean the Son of God will have healing in the corners of his garment, the *tzitzit*. "The word 'wings' used here is the same as the word 'borders' seen in Numbers 15:38. So the woman knew that if this is the Messiah, then surely if I can just get close enough to touch the hem or the borders of His garment, I can surely receive healing."[2]

By touching the edge of Jesus's cloak, the *tzitzit*, not only was she believing for healing but also she was demonstrating her belief that Jesus was the Messiah. And she was not alone in believing that she would be healed by touching Jesus's *tzitzit*. In the Gospel of Matthew, we see that multitudes of people believed this as well: "*And* when the men of that place recognized Jesus, they sent word to all the surrounding country. People brought all their sick to him and begged him to let the sick just touch the edge of his cloak, and all who touched it were healed" (Matthew 14:35-36 NIV).

The woman was bold, brave, and courageous to reach for Jesus's *tzitzit*. She had platinum faith.

PLATINUM PROJECT

You might be thinking, "I don't know if I could've stood in faith like the woman or that family. How do I ever get to the place where I totally believe and rely on the Word of God?"

In other words, how do we ever walk in platinum faith?

I think that answer is simply, when we get so full of the Word that it becomes bigger in us than any situation we're facing, then we will have moved into platinum faith.

But don't misunderstand. Platinum faith doesn't mean perfect faith; it just means "all-in" faith. We all may not walk in platinum faith every day, but we all have a measure of faith, according to the Word of God, which means we all have the potential to grow our faith to a platinum-faith level. That's good news, right?

So, here's your platinum project. Just start where you are today and ask the Lord to develop your faith. Get in the Word every day. Hang out with people who are also on this journey of faith and encourage each other, and don't quit. Eventually, you will see the victory. You will inherit the promise. You will walk in platinum faith.

DISCUSSION QUESTIONS

1. In Scripture, when David looked at Goliath, he said, "He's too big to miss." In the modern example of Tina and Clay Caldwell, they stood in faith for their daughter, Zoë, to live, despite what medical experts said. The biblical story of the woman with the bleeding issue shows someone who had exhausted all her resources for solving a problem yet believed Jesus for healing and demonstrated her belief that He was the Messiah.

   Has there been a time when you felt your faith so strong that you believed God for a certain outcome despite how circumstances may have appeared? If so, please feel free to share if you are comfortable doing so.

2. Recall a time when you felt overwhelmed and your faith was challenged. How did you react? How has your faith grown since then?

3. What are some practical steps you can take to strengthen your faith so you can stand firm when circumstances tempt to cloud your spiritual vision?

CHAPTER 2

You Are Useful

MICHELLE

*To find out what one is fitted to do, and to secure an
opportunity to do it, is the key to happiness.*

John Dewey

This was it—my fifteen-minute appointment with the editor I'd been dreaming about meeting for several months leading up to that writers conference. I'd been practicing so I felt totally ready to pitch him my women's devotional idea, but before I could begin, he started the conversation.

"So, let me understand something, Michelle," he said, peering over the top of my women's devotional proposal. "You're not pitching a children's book?"

"No, sir," I answered, smiling. "I have written and published several children's books, but I also write in other genres. In fact, I have a journalism degree and began my career writing for a daily newspaper."

"Yes, but in the Christian market you're known for your children's books."

"I guess that's true," I nodded, "but I feel like God has called me to write for women, too. That's why I have been working on this women's devotional. Would you like me tell you about it?"

I was sure he'd say yes, so I was gearing up to give my "official pitch," but I never got the chance.

"Not really," he said. "See, I think you need to understand the concept of branding. You want to be known for one specific kind of writing, not scattered over several genres. You have a real shot at making a name for yourself in the children's market, and that's not an easy genre to break into, yet you've done it successfully. Stick with that. Let someone else write women's devotionals.

Now do you have any of your little children's stories to show me?"
I swallowed hard, forced a smile, and tried to make the most
of the few minutes we had left. I did have a few children's stories
in my laptop bag, and I handed them over as he scooted the
women's devotional proposal back to me. He ended up taking my
two children's stories with him, and I was grateful for his interest
and for his words of wisdom. I knew he was genuinely trying to
help guide my career, but there was just one problem with his
branding advice—I knew God had called me to write for children
and women.

I'd heard God's voice so distinctly five years earlier during my
quiet time, sitting on my fluffy bed, while my babies napped. I was
doing one of those "read through the Bible in a year" programs,
and that day's reading was Exodus 35.

As I read about Moses and his instructions to the Israelites
concerning the construction and decorating of the tabernacle,
I read this passage about Bezalel—a master craftsman—several
times:

> *Then Moses told the people of Israel, "The LORD has*
> *specifically chosen Bezalel son of Uri, grandson of Hur,*
> *of the tribe of Judah. The LORD has filled Bezalel with the*
> *Spirit of God, giving him great wisdom, ability, and exper-*
> *tise in all kinds of crafts. He is a master craftsman, expert*
> *in working with gold, silver, and bronze. He is skilled in*
> *engraving and mounting gemstones and in carving wood.*
> *He is a master at every craft. And the LORD has given*
> *both him and Oholiab son of Ahisamach, of the tribe of*
> *Dan, the ability to teach their skills to others. The LORD*
> *has given them special skills as engravers, designers,*
> *embroiderers in blue, purple, and scarlet thread on fine*
> *linen cloth, and weavers. They excel as craftsmen and as*
> *designers." (Exodus 35:30-35 NLT)*

As I meditated on that passage, I heard God (not in that
Morgan Freeman–type voice, but in a still, small voice) say, "I

will equip you. I will guide you. I will use you. You will write for children and women and help others share their stories, all for My glory and My kingdom."

I journaled it so that I'd never forget His words to me, and I praised Him for trusting me and using me, even though at that point in my career, I hadn't yet done any of those things. I had no idea I'd ever write books, but God knew.

That's why I could appreciate that editor's advice about branding, but I couldn't follow the career path he'd suggested because God had already directed my steps. He'd impressed upon my heart that I would write for children and women and share other people's stories all for His glory. God would use me—like He used Bezalel—in more than one area. My main "craft" would be writing, but I would write in different genres. Those were my marching orders, and I was doing everything in my ability to follow them.

I still am.

You see, once I knew my purpose in life—once I knew I could be useful to the kingdom of God—I could pursue my calling with passion. I could find joy in the journey even on the days when I received nine rejection letters. (Oh yeah, it happened.) I could keep on keeping on even when the odds were stacked against me because I knew God had called me.

How about you? Have you ever had one of those "aha" moments where you knew God was speaking to you through His Word, showing you the path He has for you?

Helen Keller is credited as saying, "True happiness is not attained through self-gratification, but through fidelity to a worthy purpose."

I love that, and I believe it's true because serving God in this way makes me so happy. I can't imagine doing anything else.

So, let me ask you, what's your purpose? What's your calling? Are you walking in it? Do you feel like you're being useful in the kingdom of God?

THE COMPARISON TRAP

Romans 12:6-8 says:

> *In his grace, God has given us different gifts for doing certain things well. So if God has given you the ability to prophesy, speak out with as much faith as God has given you. If your gift is serving others, serve them well. If you are a teacher, teach well. If your gift is to encourage others, be encouraging. If it is giving, give generously. If God has given you leadership ability, take the responsibility seriously. And if you have a gift for showing kindness to others, do it gladly. (NLT)*

See, we're all created for a divine purpose. You have special giftings on the inside of you, and even if you're not using them today, they're still there! Hidden callings (ones that maybe aren't as flashy) can also be quite powerful. Think of the wind. You can't see the wind, yet it's powerful. It's always working behind the scenes, changing the topography of the land. Just because your calling isn't flashy doesn't mean it isn't far-reaching and effective. As this scripture in Romans instructs, whatever you're called to do, do it well!

Don't worry about someone else's purpose. Don't compare your calling to someone else's calling. Just focus on using your gifting well. Run your race, and finish in faith!

But that's easier said than done, isn't it? I get it. You look at someone else's calling; you see your friend being used in a mighty way; and then you look at what God's called you to do; and you fall into the comparison trap. So, rather than dwell in the desolate land of comparison, you grab a package of Oreos, head for the couch, and binge on Netflix for many hours. (Yes, I've done it, too, only I usually opt for chocolate chip cookies.)

There's a better way.

Put those cookies back in the snack drawer and listen to me: you are important in the body of Christ. Whether God is using you mightily as a stay-at-home mom or profoundly as an inspirational speaker in venues around the world, your purpose is paramount. One calling isn't more special than the other. Sure, one might be more behind the scenes than the other, but both callings are useful to God. What if you're parenting a little girl who grows up to make a difference in the world—maybe even cure cancer? What you do—what each one of us does—is important to the kingdom of God.

First Corinthians 12:14-27 says:

> *Yes, the body has many different parts, not just one part. If the foot says, "I am not a part of the body because I am not a hand," that does not make it any less a part of the body. And if the ear says, "I am not part of the body because I am not an eye," would that make it any less a part of the body? If the whole body were an eye, how would you hear? Or if your whole body were an ear, how would you smell anything?*
>
> *But our bodies have many parts, and God has put each part just where he wants it. How strange a body would be if it had only one part! Yes, there are many parts, but only one body. The eye can never say to the hand, "I don't need you." The head can't say to the feet, "I don't need you."*
>
> *In fact, some parts of the body that seem weakest and least important are actually the most necessary. And the parts we regard as less honorable are those we clothe with the greatest care. So we carefully protect those parts that should not be seen, while the more honorable parts do not require this special care. So God has put the body together such that extra honor and care are given to those parts that have less dignity. This makes for harmony among the members, so that all the members care for each other. If one part suffers, all the parts suffer with it, and if one part is honored, all the parts are glad.*
>
> *All of you together are Christ's body, and each of you is a part of it. (NLT)*

That's right. Each one of us serves a different purpose. Each one of us is part of the body of Christ. And, each one of us is useful. But in order to be useful for God, we have to understand and accept our calling, and then we have to step out of our comfort zones and let God use us in great and mighty ways.

That's why we can't fall into that comparison trap. Instead of comparing your calling to your flashy friend's calling, celebrate her calling! Rejoice that God is using her in such a dynamic way! When you can finally do that with a genuine heart, you might find that God is also using you in some amazing ways and now that your attention is on Him, you can focus on His calling for *your* life.

That takes platinum faith.

Live Brilliant:

Smoke-Detector Seasons

BETHANY

When Justin was a youth minister, I dreamed of him being on stage speaking to hundreds of students. I saw myself working his table at events, behind the scenes, happy to be the supportive wife. But when I shared my dreams for him, Justin always said, "I don't want to be that guy." And I never understood why.

I never understood until God whispered in my ear: "You're projecting My dreams for you onto him."

As a youth minister's wife and stay-at-home mom, I didn't see how that was possible. I hadn't finished my bachelor's degree at that time, and I wasn't planning on joining the workforce anytime soon. My passion was teens and college-aged students, but how was I supposed to become the main event?

I considered my role as Chief Supportive Officer.

And for a time, it was.

Until it wasn't.

I almost didn't attend the writers conference in 2012.

Who was I to think anyone would publish me?

And yet God uses the weak and uninformed and completely unqualified to share His message. I left that conference with the Writer of the Year award, signed with an agent the next week, and sold my first book to a publisher three months later. It was truly a Cinderella-esque experience.

Our seasons of being the smoke detector are important, but they're not always meant to be our role of the lifetime. I needed to be the support for Justin's ministry, which I considered to be 100 percent my ministry, too. Otherwise I wouldn't have been in the trenches or had the firsthand experience to be able to write my first young adult book for girls about dating and confidence.

I was afraid to step out of my role. Afraid to step into the spotlight. Afraid to be vocal.

But the thing about smoke detectors is this: they're the most useful when they're making noise.

PLATINUM PROPERTY

Of all the metals, platinum is one of the most useful. In fact, "it is estimated that one-fifth of everything we use today either contains platinum or requires platinum in its manufacturing."[1] Platinum is used in everything from catalytic converters to high-end jewelry pieces. Did you know that platinum is also used in pacemakers, in aural and retinal implants, and for its anti-cancer elements in cancer-fighting drugs?[2]

Here's a short list of additional ways platinum is used today:

- To make high-temperature thermocouples
- To make optically pure, flat glass for TVs, LCDs, and monitors
- To make threads of glass for fiber optics
- To form the tips of automotive and aeronautic spark plugs
- As a substitute for gold in electronic connections
- In coatings for ceramic capacitors in electronic devices
- In dental implants
- To make high-quality flutes
- In smoke and carbon monoxide detectors
- To manufacture silicones
- In coatings for razors[3]

Before we began researching platinum (when we were choosing the name of our business, Platinum Literary), I had no idea this precious metal had so many different uses. When I thought of platinum, I thought of diamonds set in this gorgeous white-hot metal. And, in my defense, some sources indicate that more than 40 percent of all wedding rings sold in the United States contain some platinum.[4] But, to think this metal is also used in pacemakers and cancer-fighting drugs? That was news to me. Yet, according to several sources, platinum-based drugs (platins) have been used for over forty years to fight cancer.

Platinum has so many important uses! Do you think the platinum used in dental implants is any less important than the platinum used in retinal implants? No, because both are necessary and needed. It's the same with us, as members of the body of Christ. Our different callings are needed. One isn't better than the other. All are needed or God wouldn't have given us our specific individual callings.

Here's where it gets tough. Let's say your best friend's calling is more like the platinum that goes into a $75,000 wedding set—shiny, exquisite, and expensive. And, your calling is more like the platinum that goes into a smoke detector—hidden yet necessary. Let's face it: sometimes it hurts to be the smoke detector. Just because your friend's calling is going to be celebrated and out front for all to see while your calling is hidden and less exciting, does that devalue your calling? Absolutely not. In fact, your calling saves lives!

PLATINUM PROMISE

That comparison trap has been around for a long time, and it usually plays out as devastating jealousy and rage. Remember the story of David and King Saul found in 1 Samuel? Let's look at a short passage together:

> When the victorious Israelite army was returning home after David had killed the Philistine, women from all the towns of Israel came out to meet King Saul. They sang and danced for joy with tambourines and cymbals. This was their song: "Saul has killed his thousands, and David his ten thousands!" This made Saul very angry. "What's this?" he said. "They credit David with ten thousands and me with only thousands. Next they'll be making him their king!" So from that time on Saul kept a jealous eye on David. The very next day a tormenting spirit from God overwhelmed Saul, and he began to rave in his house like a madman. David was playing the harp, as he did each day. But Saul had a spear in his hand, and he suddenly hurled

it at David, intending to pin him to the wall. But David
escaped him twice. (1 Samuel 18:6-11 NLT)

As you might imagine, Saul was not pleased when the women danced and sang, "Saul has killed his thousands, and David his ten thousands!" That was a slap in the face to King Saul, and he wasn't having it. He couldn't stand the fact that David was being recognized and praised above him. That was the beginning of the end of David and Saul's relationship and ultimately the end of Saul's relationship with God. Saul slipped into that comparison trap and allowed jealousy and bitterness to take root in his heart, and before long, he was hurling spears at David and hunting him down like an animal.

And, here's the thing. What the women were singing wasn't even accurate! Saul was a great warrior king who had won many battles, and all of David's military exploits were in service to Saul. So, you might say that David's victories were Saul's victories. Even so, Saul was jealous of David's fame and recognized that God was with David. In other words, Saul recognized the call upon David's life, and he just couldn't deal with it. Eventually, Saul dies in battle, and David is anointed king.

Take it from Saul, comparing yourself and your calling to another person and his calling doesn't end well. Instead, use that same energy to follow the path God has for you. Stay focused on Him and His calling upon your life. Because once you know your calling and you walk in that calling, joy that only comes from the Lord will fill you up.

Ever since I heard from God concerning the call upon my life—to write for Him—I've been settled in my spirit. That anxious, all-consuming drive to make a name for myself disappeared, and God replaced it with a desire to honor His Name. No, every day hasn't been butterflies and sunshine and bluebirds on my shoulder, but every day I've been aware of the call and grateful that God could use me.

I want the same peace for you. I want you to experience the kind of joy that only comes from following the plan God has for your life and letting Him use you in mighty ways.

PLATINUM PROJECT

If you feel lost today because you're a little foggy on your calling, you're not alone. For thousands of years people have pondered the question: "Why am I here?" Some never find the answer to that question because they look in the wrong places. The world doesn't hold that answer; only God does.

Pastor and author Rick Warren explained it this way:

> The easiest way to discover the purpose of an invention is to ask the creator of it. The same is true for discovering your life's purpose: ask God . . . God's purpose for your life is far greater than your own personal fulfillment, your peace of mind, or even your happiness. It will last longer than your family, your ministry, or even your dreams and ambitions. To know why you were placed on this planet, you must begin with God. You were born by His purpose and for His purpose.[5]

He's not trying to keep this crucial calling information from you, so take some time this week to seek Him. Spend time in His Word. And, pray: "Father God, I know You have a divine purpose for my life, and I don't want to walk outside my calling. I want to walk smack-dab in the middle of it. I want to be useful in Your kingdom. Use me, Lord. I am asking for Your wisdom and direction as I step out in faith to serve You. Thank You, God, for choosing me and using me. In the Mighty Name of Your Son Jesus. Amen."

Ephesians 1:11 says, "In him we were also chosen, having been predestined according to the plan of him who works out everything in conformity with the purpose of his will" (NIV).

God will work out His plan for your life according to His will. All you have to do is stay close to Him. I believe that even today, you'll begin to get cues from your Heavenly Father. Just sit in His presence and have your journal handy as you listen. Prayer is a two-way street. You can't do all of the talking. You need to sit quietly before Him so He can talk to you. You might be thinking, "I'm pretty sure I've never heard God's voice before, so how will I know it's Him?" The Word says that "my sheep know my voice" (John 10:27 CEV), and if you're born again, you are a sheep and He is your shepherd, and you'll know His voice.

As I look back on my life, I realize that God left me bread crumbs in my quest to find my calling. I knew in first grade I wanted to be a writer. How did I know? Well, I won a poetry contest and realized I was actually good at something, because let me tell you, I was struggling in math. (I still do! Thank goodness I married a CPA who is a genius with numbers.)

My poem went a little something like this: "Penny is my very best friend. I'll love her to the very end. She's a very special wiener dog. I love her though she smells like a hog."

OK, so I wasn't exactly a first-grade Dr. Seuss, but my poem was good enough to earn first prize. (I guess the other first-grade poets must've been really bad.) At any rate, I won a few sparkly pencils and the honor of going first in the lunch line that afternoon. My teacher also displayed my poem in the front of the room for all to see. I stared at my winning poem all afternoon.

That's the day I *thought* I became a writer, but actually I was born a writer because that calling was upon me when I was in my mother's womb. And, so was your calling. It's always been in you and on you, whether you're walking in it today or not. So, look back over your life for those bread crumbs. What has brought you the greatest joy in life? Was it when you were working with the teenagers at your church? Or was it when you were volunteering at the women's shelter? Is there something in your life that no matter how many times you've walked away from it or tried to deny it, that "thing" keeps coming back around? Think back. Have people in your life been confirming your calling throughout your life, but you hadn't realized it until this very moment?

That's your platinum project today: spend some time asking God to show you the answer to those questions and either reveal your calling for the first time or confirm your purpose in an amazing way. And, don't be surprised if you feel your calling is too big or that you're not qualified to fulfill it. You don't have to be qualified; you just have to answer the call because God will equip you. So, use some of that platinum faith and step out of your comfort zone and into your calling.

DISCUSSION QUESTIONS

1. We're all created for a special purpose, yet it is so easy to compare ourselves with others. In Scripture, Saul was jealous of David's fame and recognized God was with David. Saul just couldn't deal with it and eventually died in battle. How can we learn from Saul's mistake and avoid the comparison trap?

2. Bethany referred to a "smoke-detector season" when she was afraid to step into the spotlight, although this time laid the foundation for her first project as an author. Have you ever been in a smoke-detector season? How did it lay the groundwork for your purpose?

3. What has brought you the greatest joy in life? Is there something in your life that, no matter how many times you've walked away from it or tried to deny it, keeps coming back around? Chances are, it points to your purpose. If you are still unsure, ask your sisters in Christ to join with you in prayer for clarity.

CHAPTER 3

You Can Withstand the Heat

BETHANY

Our wretched species is so made that those who walk on the well-trodden path always throw stones at those who are showing a new road.

Voltaire

Have you ever been in a situation in which you know you're doing what God has called you to do but there seems to be opposition at every corner? Have you ever felt like you were holding on to the end of your rope, and if one more thing happened, you'd be left empty-handed?

When we find ourselves in these situations, it's important for us to look at it through a lens of the physical (what's actually happening to us) as well as the spiritual (could there be more to the story than what is seen?).

Currently the opposition I'm facing has to do with my hands, the instruments I use to tell stories, share content, and write books. For the past three years I've been dealing with severe dryness on my fingertips. My skin issues didn't start until we moved to Mississippi, smack-dab in the middle of ghostwriting a book called *Through the Eyes of Hope* and in the middle of the first full year of my new company Serious Writer. I always blamed the situation because the first crack on my hand came after the eight-hour drive the day we moved. I thought it was from holding the steering wheel for so long. But the day after it healed, my fingers started to peel, so I blamed the physical location of Biloxi and didn't even think to look at the spiritual side of what was happening in my life.

The heat was turning up.

PLATINUM PROPERTY

One of the awesome properties of platinum is its ability to withstand super high temperatures. Its melting point is over

3000°F, which is higher than that of titanium, silver, and gold.[1] This characteristic makes platinum an ideal metal for protecting other metals—they can withstand higher temperatures when surrounded by a platinum covering.

In the same way, our Heavenly Father protects us so that we can face hard situations, that is, "face the heat." When we are faced with attacks from the enemy, it is not our strength that protects us, but God's. Second Thessalonians 3:3 says, "But the Lord is faithful, and he will strengthen you and protect you from the evil one" (NIV).

Strengthen and protect.

That's platinum love.

We cannot withstand the evil one on our own. He is more powerful than we are, and let's be honest here—he's not flesh and blood. He's not mortal. He does not have a soul. He was not created in God's image. Satan is not our equal.

He's *not* our equal.

We are weaker than him, but our God is stronger and our God fights for us and protects us from the enemy that roams the earth and seeks to devour us (see 1 Peter 5:8).

When we become a Christian we receive the gift of the Holy Spirit. We are shielded inside where it matters most: our soul.

When Satan attacked Job, he wasn't allowed to touch the essence of who Job was, only his body, belongings, and beloveds.

That's what he does to us.

If you're ever unsure of what God's call on your life is, think about where you face the most adversity, the most heat.

Satan will attack us where it hurts the most.

PLATINUM PROMISE

The part of you that God wants to use for His glory is exactly where the enemy is likely to attack. You may not even be aware of where God wants to use you—so pay attention to where the attacks are directed. We must pray for protection against those fiery arrows, but even then sometimes God allows them to hit their mark.

The story of Shadrach, Meshach, and Abednego is more than three guys being thrown into the fiery furnace. The text indicates that their peers turned them in for not worshipping the statue: "At this time some astrologers came forward and denounced the Jews. . . . Your majesty issued a decree. . . . But there are some Jews whom you have set over the affairs of the province of Babylon—Shadrach, Meshach and Abednego—who pay no attention to you, Your Majesty. They neither serve your gods nor worship the image of gold you have set up" (Daniel 3:8-10, 12 NIV).

Grown-ups still tattle.

Jealously isn't a modern issue. Even in biblical times it got people into trouble.

The Babylonians conquered the Jewish people, yet Daniel and his three friends were singled out for their faith and desire to do what is right in the sight of the one true God. They didn't eat the food of the palace, instead requesting a special vegetarian diet, which might be our first biblical instance where a chef wishes they'd instilled a "no substitutions" policy for the menu.

As the story goes, the four friends were given ten days to eat their special diet instead of the rich foods of the palace. At the end of the week-and-a-half experiment, there was a visible difference between Daniel and his buddies and the other young men with them (see Daniel 1:6-20).

From the very beginning, Daniel, Shadrach, Meshach, and Abednego were favored. The Bible says that "to these four young men God gave knowledge and understanding of all kinds of literature and learning" (Daniel 1:17 NIV).

When God places a divine calling on your life, He sees you through the obstacles. God protected their bodies when they first arrived; and when they were faced with death, God protected them again.

King Nebuchadnezzar is hot when the three men (Daniel is not mentioned) refused to bow down to the ninety-foot-tall statue he'd erected. The threat of death is imminent: Nebuchadnezzar threatened them with being burned alive if they didn't comply and ordered the furnace to be hotter than usual. But the response of these three brave platinum-faith men is still one of my favorites in all of the Bible.

In my mind, I see them square their shoulders as the sound of the furnace roars in their ears. Could they feel the heat from where they were standing? Was Nebuchadnezzar close enough for them to feel his hot breath on their cheeks?

"We don't have to defend ourselves to you, O king," they said (my paraphrase).

That's a bit cheeky in the English translation.

They continued. "Our God can save us from that fiery furnace and He can rescue us from you." *They were, don't forget, Jews captured by the Babylonian people.*

And now for my favorite part.

"But even if He does not [save or rescue us], we want you to know that we won't worship your gods or the image you set up."

If Nebuchadnezzar wasn't mad before, he was furious now.

The furnace was ordered seven times hotter than it was.

Seven: the number of spiritual perfection.[2]

The flames licked the sides of the furnace and reached for the men, gobbling up the soldiers whose unfortunate task was to escort Shadrach, Meshach, and Abednego to their death. But instead of dying, they stood in the furnace with a fourth man, whom many theologians believe to be Jesus, or rather, the pre-incarnate Christ.

Nebuchadnezzar couldn't believe his eyes. All four were walking around unbound. The flames that burned their bonds left their skin untouched. In fact, when Nebuchadnezzar ordered their removal from the furnace, the men weren't singed and had no smell of smoke upon them.

To not even smell like smoke is truly an act of God. When we lived in South Tampa, there was an amazing hole-in-the-wall bar that served the best wings you'll ever taste. Their mouth-watering homemade sauces should truly be bottled and sold in stores. The bar was so smoke-filled that Justin would come home with a takeout order and need to shower immediately because the smoke clung to his clothes, hair, and skin.

At the very least, Shadrach, Meshach, and Abednego should have smelled like a barbeque.

What we know is this: the God of Shadrach, Meshach, and Abednego is the same God we serve today. And while we may never be faced with a fiery physical death, we may encounter some hot situations and need to call upon Him for protection.

And even if He does not save us at the moment we want Him to, we trust that His plans are greater than ours and believe with a platinum faith that He will work out all things for His glory and His purpose.

Prevent and Protect When Possible

Even after I finished the ghostwriting project and we moved to Biloxi, my hands remained irritated. The skin was cracked, even into the nail beds, and in several places the dermis and hypodermis were exposed. Many times they'd bleed. Typing became painful, and soaps and cleaning products became unbearable.

My husband complained about a paper cut one day, and in an uncompassionate moment, I told him to imagine having fifty that never went away.

That was my life: bleeding fingers and Band-Aids.

Until Dr. T.

Dr. T is an older gentleman with a quick smile and faster wit. He held my hands face up, examining the ugly fissures and bright red blood spots.

"Look at those healthy pinkies!" he said, and I felt hope for the first time in almost three years. Doctor after doctor dismissed the dry, cracked skin on my fingers as a simple dermatitis, and one doctor ran tests for autoimmune diseases (negative). But by the grace of God, Dr. T was willing to find the source of this skin condition.

"You're right-handed, aren't you?" asked Dr. T.

"Yes," I answered. My watch is on my left wrist, opposite of my writing hand, and most people are right-handed so I wasn't sure why he asked.

"Look here," he said, pointing at the red line running from the top of my pointer finger down the side of soft skin to the webbing by my thumb. "This is a strange line, but it tells me, along with the cracking and peeling on your thumbs and first two fingers, that you're holding something primarily in this hand."

"And see," he continued, "your pinkies and ring fingers are unaffected."

He released my hands with a gentle squeeze and leaned back on the little round cushioned stool.

"We've got to figure out what's causing that allergy."

After an extensive patch test that required a full test panel of common allergens applied in a grid on my back, taped from side to side, and strict instructions to not shower or get wet for forty-eight hours, I couldn't wait to find out the results.

Part of my back started itching the moment they applied the patches, but I couldn't scratch or move the tape in any way in case it messed up the results.

On the second day, I sat in the patient chair while the nurse removed the tape. "Whoa—that one popped!"

Popped?

"That area itches really badly," I said.

"I'm sure it does," she replied. She gently peeled off the rest of the tape and patches. "Your skin didn't like that tape," she said. "Let's see what that big reaction was to."

She checked her chart and under her breath she said, "Huh."

"It's colophony," she said. "The doctor will know what that is, but I don't."

I didn't either.

#Google.

Colophony, also known as bow resin, comes from the sap of coniferous trees and is found in *tons* of everyday items and has a wide use in paper manufacturing.

Paper.

As I am an author, homeschool mom, booklover, journaler, and Happy Planner addict, this was terrible news. Colophony is in newspaper, photo paper, magazine paper, inks, stickers, adhesives, tapes (which is why the tape outline was bright red and itchy from the testing), paper with any type of waterproofing like labels, and about one hundred other things.

And regular printing paper? Gives my skin friction burns.

The cure?

None known at this time.

The treatment?

Prevention and protection. Prevent yourself from touching anything with colophony in it. Protect your hands when you do.

PREVENT THE HEAT IF POSSIBLE

When it comes to having platinum faith, our goal and desire needs to be that we live in such a way that is above reproach, so that even our enemies will be ashamed to say anything against us (see Titus 2:8).

Don't kill anyone? Got it. I'm good there.

Live above reproach? That's a bit harder.

The Bible says that we should avoid not just evil, but the *appearance* of evil (see 1 Thessalonians 5:22), which, if I may say, is much harder than not doing evil at all because some people will always disagree with your life choices.

Seriously, when it comes to sin, some things are obvious and spelled out: don't kill each other. Other things can fall into a grey area called conviction, where Scripture doesn't speak against something but suggests it might not be the best idea.

Romans 14:21 says it's better to not do something if it makes your Christian brother or sister stumble. We must be careful to pay attention to each other, to support each other, and to be self-less. Doing whatever we want just because we *can* isn't the way to live.

I yell at my kids sometimes. I occasionally disrespect my husband. I say words that aren't *really* curse words but kind of have the same meaning to get my point across, *dang it.*

When our goal is to be like Jesus, to live in a way that we honor God in everything we do, we have to ask God to show us those dirty little cracks in our hearts where we cause someone to stumble and show us the things we do that have the appearance of evil.

Because sometimes, if I'm being truthful, I don't want to know where those little crevices of sin are hiding. What this says to me is that while my spirit is willing, because yes, God, I want to be holy, my flesh is weak and I need to submit to Jesus's teaching and commit myself to prayer (see Matthew 26:41).

THE POWER OF AVOIDANCE

It's hard not to touch an item made with colophony because colophony is not a required ingredient for companies to list. It's always a gamble, and I always lose.

Recently, the "gripping area" of my right hand was starting to crack and peel, signs that a full-on skin disaster was about to happen.

But I had no idea what I'd touched.

I could tell from the skin pattern that it was something I'd held in my hand, like a cup or a book. But it wasn't until I reached for my water bottle to take a sip that I put two-and-two together.

The label sits exactly where the bottle is cradled into my hand and exactly where I could now see the fresh pink soft underbelly of my fingers that should never be exposed.

To prevent these accidental brushes with scary paper, I have to wear gloves. So sexy.

Since I spend the majority of my day on my laptop or using my phone, I need gloves that are thin enough to allow me to type and will respond to the touchscreen sensors. After testing multiple brands and various sizes, I found my favorite brand of gloves, designed for hair dressers, and not only do they come in a sleek black with extended cuff, but they also make a version in pink. Yay!

The gloves do more than prevent colophony touching my fingers; they also protect them. Despite breakout after breakout, I tend to repeat the same insane cycle: my hands crack and peel, I wear gloves 24/7, my hands heal, I touch things without gloves, my hands crack and peel.

And because I can't seem to learn my lesson, my fingers are almost always cracked.

This blooms into a fresh nightmare: open wounds are bull's-eye targets for germs.

While preventing the cracked skin is important, it's vital to protect it.

Growing up in church, I often heard references to God's "umbrella of protection." The idea is that God covers us with His protection as long as we stay within the safety boundaries, just like an umbrella protects us from the elements if we stay underneath its cover. And similar to how we'll get soaked if we step outside the umbrella's shelter, we risk getting hurt when we stray from God's path.

But the Bible doesn't really suggest that if we are righteous and stay in God's will, that we won't get hurt.

In fact, it's often the people who are doing God's will who get hurt the most.

Stephen was preaching to the Romans when Paul (then Saul) had him stoned to death (see Acts 7:54-60).

Job was a righteous man, and Satan attacked him in every way but death (see the book of Job).

Jesus was doing His Father's will and suffered the most terrible and agonizing death, including taking our sins onto His shoulders and experiencing our punishment for those sins.

There seems to be a lot of death involved.

So can we really protect ourselves? Self-preservation is instinctive. Natural. When we have children, we extend this instinct into protecting them from everything: sharp corners, large chunks of food, and well-meaning strangers who want to pinch their cheeks.

We understand how to protect ourselves physically and will sometimes go to great expense to do so. But when it comes to the spiritual, which is the greater of the two, do we go to great expense to guard our hearts?

Do we speak words of Scripture over ourselves and over our families?

Do we fill our hearts with Bible verses so that the Holy Spirit can bring them to mind at exactly the right second?

Do we avoid situations that are temptation black holes?

Do we confess our sins to each other so that we might be saved (see James 5:16)?

These are the ways we build a platinum faith that withstands the heat.

Live Brilliant:
Prayers of Protection

MICHELLE

It's important to pray protection over ourselves and our loved ones. But if you aren't sure how to pray powerful prayers, here are a few tips to help you.

1. Always begin your prayer with praise to God. For example, say: "Father, we praise You that You'll never leave us nor forsake us. We love You so much."

2. Be specific with your requests. For example, don't just pray for protection over your loved ones. Instead, pray specifically as it pertains to the situation such as: "God, I ask that you protect my spouse today as he travels for work. I pray that Your angels surround his vehicle and that he arrives home safely without delay."

3. Use scripture in your prayers. So, instead of praying, "Lord, I ask that you protect me from the office rumors," pray, "Lord, I thank You that no weapon formed against me shall prosper and every tongue that rises against me shall be stilled." (Remember, Jeremiah 1:12 tells us that God watches over His Word to perform it.)

4. Believe when you pray. Don't just say the words; believe that God can really answer your requests. Pray expecting! After you've made your request known to God, thank Him for the desired result. Hebrews 11:6 says, "It's impossible to please God apart from faith. And why? Because anyone who wants to approach God must believe both that he exists and that he cares enough to respond to those who seek him" (MSG). Also, check out Matthew 21:22 and Mark 11:24. Of course, His response might not be the answer we desire, but we have to trust Him enough to believe He has our best interest at heart. Remember that Garth Brooks song that said, "I thank God for unanswered prayers." So do I. In fact, I often pray, "Lord, this is what I'm believing you to do in this situation, but I know You see the beginning to the end, so I trust You in all of this. If that door needs to be closed, then close it."

5. Pray in Jesus's Name. The Bible clearly tells us to pray in Jesus's Name. In John 16:23, Jesus says: "And in that day you will ask Me nothing. Most assuredly, I say to you, whatever you ask the Father in My name He will give you" (NKJV).

So, with all of those things in mind, here's an example of a prayer of protection:

"Father, I praise You that You are my twenty-four-hour, seven-days-a-week God and that You are my refuge in times of trouble. Your Word says that You are a wall of fire round about me and that Your angels surround me. Thank You for those promises! Father God, I know that You can see all things and that You know the future. Thank You that I can trust You. I do not walk in fear because I know that You have me in the palm of Your hand—even in the midst of trials and tribulations. Hallelujah! In Jesus's Mighty Name, Amen."

Live Brilliant:

Protection Promises

You are my hiding place; you will protect me from trouble and surround me with songs of deliverance. (Psalm 32:7 NIV)

God is our refuge and strength, an ever-present help in trouble. (Psalm 46:1 NIV)

You make your saving help my shield, and your right hand sustains me; your help has made me great. You provide a broad path for my feet, so that my ankles do not give way. (Psalm 18:35-36 NIV)

"No weapon forged against you will prevail, and you will refute every tongue that accuses you. This is the heritage of the servants of the Lord, and this is their vindication from me," declares the Lord.
(Isaiah 54:17 NIV)

Keep me safe, my God, for in you I take refuge.
(Psalm 16:1 NIV)

The Lord will fight for you; you need only to be still. (Exodus 14:14 NIV)

The Lord is with me; I will not be afraid. What can mere mortals do to me? (Psalm 118:6 NIV)

You are my refuge and my shield; I have put my hope in your word. (Psalm 119:114 NIV)

"And I myself will be a wall of fire around it," declares the LORD, "and I will be its glory within." (Zechariah 2:5 NIV)

The angel of the LORD encamps around those who fear him, and he delivers them. (Psalm 34:7 NIV)

As for God, his way is perfect: The LORD's word is flawless; he shields all who take refuge in him. (Psalm 18:30 NIV)

PLATINUM PROJECT

We all have our own fiery furnaces to deal with.

Sometimes the blaze is bright and burns quickly.

Other times it spreads slowly and turns everything it touches to ash.

When life gets tough, it's important to remember that God is in control. He sees us, loves us, and is with us always. He never leaves us.

Memorize the verses about God's protection and meditate on them day and night (Joshua 1:8). Keep a prayer diary. The Happy Planner Mini makes a perfectly sized journal to record your requests and God's answers. He proves to us that He is always there—even when the fire is lapping at our ankles and we're afraid we'll get burned—and that by His grace we can withstand the heat.

DISCUSSION QUESTIONS

1. The enemy is most likely to attack you in the area where God wants to use you for His glory. In the Old Testament, Daniel and his three friends were singled out for their faith, with the three friends being placed in a fiery furnace as a result. When they entered the furnace, they had platinum faith that God's will would be done, whatever the outcome. If you had been in their situation, how might you have reacted?

2. Standing on God's promises gives us strength in situations when our faith is tested. Have you been in a situation where you relied on God's promises to bring you through it? If so, feel free to share the promise with others so they, too, can embed it in their hearts.

3. Scripture encourages us to live in a way where we honor God in all things. Since we are only human, how would this be possible?

CHAPTER 4

You Are Precious

MICHELLE

*God has formed many diamonds. But He made only one
you. You are unique.*

Darlene Sala

We'd been putting it off for months. It was time. With both daughters home for the weekend, my husband, Jeff, and I knew it was the perfect day to go through his late mama's house. Nana, as we lovingly called her, had passed unexpectedly in September 2017, leaving a large house full of furniture, every kitchen gadget known to man, three closets jam-packed with clothes, and a big hole in our hearts.

We adored her.

But you know who wouldn't have adored her?

Marie Kondo of the hit show *Tidying Up*.

Though Nana kept an impeccable house, she was a bit of a pack rat. And if you know anything about Kondo, who has written four books on the art of organizing and de-cluttering, she preaches against "pack-ratting" or saving anything that doesn't "spark joy."

As we made our way through every closet and drawer, I was amazed. Nana had kept every single newspaper clipping about Jeff's glory days as a running back for our local high school. In fact, she'd kept his football jerseys all the way back to his first venture onto the field. It was such a tiny jersey! We also found all of his report cards, graded papers, pictures he'd colored, and art projects he'd completed—including a scary ceramic rabbit (at least we think it was a rabbit) with his initials etched on the bottom.

Jeff was an only child. His mama loved him dearly, and I'm

guessing she would've fought hard to keep every single memento that celebrated her precious son if Kondo had been summoned to her house for an episode of *Tidying Up!* Because to Nana, even the ugly ceramic rabbit was a priceless masterpiece because it'd been given to her by a blue-eyed little boy who adored his mama. We tend to hold onto things that are of sentimental value, and that's why in Kondo's method of decluttering, the sentimental stuff is the last category to tackle—because it's often the hardest.

YOU ARE PRICELESS

After my father, Walter Medlock, passed away, my sister and I agreed to help Mom sort through his personal items. As we divided up the tasks to be accomplished, I quickly volunteered to tackle the master bedroom. Of course, I had an ulterior motive: I wanted to go through Daddy's special drawer. You see, it was the one drawer he wouldn't allow anyone to bother.

Even though he was almost deaf in one ear, Daddy could hear you opening that drawer from a mile away. I remember as a kid trying to quietly ease it open in order to sneak some quarters from his big bowl of change. (I wanted to feed the *Pac-Man* game at the local arcade.) As I would start to reach my hand inside, I'd hear, "Michelle Leigh Medlock, are you in my drawer?" He didn't mind giving me money for *Pac-Man*—he just didn't want me rifling through his stuff.

For years, I'd wondered what could possibly be in that forbidden treasure trove.

"I'll start in Daddy's chest of drawers," I called to my mom. As I searched through Daddy's things, I found very ordinary items. His comb. Fingernail clippers. His money clip. Pictures of the family. Lots of change. Some "I owe you" notes that my sister and I had left over the years when we'd borrow a few quarters. His special engraved calculator he used in business. And a lockbox.

I was just about to ask Mom if she knew the combination to the lockbox, but I thought I'd try forcing it open first. Surprisingly, it wasn't actually locked and popped right open with just a little pressure. I don't know what I expected to be inside the lockbox in Daddy's special drawer—diamonds, maybe? stock in Apple? keys to another lockbox that contained the real treasure?

But I didn't find any of those things.

Inside, I discovered important documents like his and my mother's marriage license, a small wooden Bible, a Jesus Saves lapel pin, and three tiny plastic bracelets—two pink and one blue. The wording had yellowed over the years, but I could still read the faint printing.

"Medlock Girl," I mouthed as I read the words. And, there was more. My birthdate was printed next to "Medlock Girl" on one of the pink bracelets; my sister's birthday was printed on the other pink one; and the blue bracelet said "Medlock Boy" with my brother's birthdate! I held that tiny pink bracelet close to my heart for what seemed like hours.

I'd always known my father loved me, but it was at that exact moment I realized just how much my Daddy treasured me. As I held that little pink bracelet, I knew I was priceless. To Walter Medlock, I was worth more than all of the platinum in the world! He loved me so much that he even treasured that faded, peeling thirty-five-year-old baby bracelet.

Even now as I share this story with you, I am overcome with feelings of love. You see, I knew how much my earthly father loved me and valued me, and those feelings of being treasured have remained in my heart even though my father has been in heaven more than fourteen years. I think that's why I've never had a difficult time receiving the unconditional love of my Heavenly Father. I know in my knower that God loves and values me even more than my earthly father did. What about you? Do you have that same confidence that your Heavenly Father loves and cherishes you? Because here's the thing—until you believe that God adores you, you won't be able to trust Him. And trusting Him is essential to walking in platinum faith.

If you didn't have a daddy as wonderful as Walter Medlock, you may be struggling to accept your Heavenly Father's love. You may not realize how precious you are to God, so let me enlighten you a bit. You have a Heavenly Father who treasures you, and He has little plastic bracelets—His promises of love—all throughout His Word. Every time you find one—like Jeremiah 31:3 that says, "I have loved you with an everlasting love"—you'll want to hold it close to your heart, just like I did. Need more convincing that God adores you and considers you priceless?

Luke 12:6-7 says, "What is the price of five sparrows—two copper coins? Yet God does not forget a single one of them. And the very hairs on your head are all numbered. So don't be afraid; you are more valuable to God than a whole flock of sparrows" (NLT).

God flat loves you!

He adores you!

You are precious to Him!

PLATINUM PROPERTY

Speaking of precious, platinum is what we call a "precious metal." According to Merriam-Webster, a precious metal is defined as any of the less common and highly valuable metals such as gold, silver, and the platinum metals.[1] And, of those precious metals, platinum is one of the rarest. In fact, according to some sources, about 2,800 tons of gold is produced every year compared to only 250 tons of platinum.[2] One expert said, "Platinum is much rarer than both gold and silver—so rare, in fact, that all of the Platinum ever mined could fit into your living room."[3] Another source said that platinum is fifteen times more scarce than gold.

Now, I don't know if those statements are 100 percent accurate, but regardless, platinum is precious and rare, and that makes it very valuable.

YOU ARE VALUABLE

When we think about something being valuable here on earth, we can trace that value back to three things:

1. Its rarity
2. The amount someone is willing to pay for it
3. The previous owner

Let's tackle number one—rarity. Sometimes called *scarcity value*, rarity leads to a higher unit price. For example, the 1963 Ferrari 250 GTO is supposedly the most expensive car in the world, valued at approximately $52 million. Sure, it's a vintage Italian sports car, but that's not why it's worth so much money.[4] Here's the real reason—only thirty-six of the Ferrari 250 GTO were ever made. Now, that's rare! And, that's expensive.

Speaking of Ferraris, when I was sixteen, my parents surprised me with a brand-new red Pontiac Fiero. They were two-seaters, made of plastic, and I thought they were the cutest cars ever! So, I was pretty excited when I became the proud owner of a lipstick red 1986 Fiero. Even though it was a pretty inexpensive car—definitely not luxury—I loved it. As I pulled up to our local Jiffy Treet on my first Fiero outing, the man working the drive-through said, "Wow! That's a beautiful Ferrari!" As he hurried off to retrieve my Diet Cherry Pepsi with extra ice, I remember smiling really big and thinking, "As much as I love this car, it might as well be a Ferrari."

But I digress.

OK, let's move on to number two—the amount someone is willing to pay. It's the second criteria that determines the value of something. Let's take Christian Louboutin's trademark red-bottomed shoes, for example. A pair of those status stilettos starts at $695, and the most expensive pair sells for about $6,000. When *The New York Times* asked Louboutin why his shoes were so costly, he explained it was quite expensive to make shoes in Europe, noting that his company's production cost had greatly increased as the euro strengthened against the dollar. Others who love these red-soled stunners add that the incredible craftsmanship and expensive materials (rhinestones, feathers, and so on) up the price. But, bottom line, the reason Louboutin can sell his shoes for so much money is because the demand is there; celebrities and wealthy individuals around the globe want them, and they're willing to pay big bucks for them.[5]

If I spray-painted the soles of my favorite black pointed-toe heels with that signature red color, could I sell them for $695? Probably not, because there's not a demand for Michelle Medlock Adams's stilettos. But if they were Louboutin's, celebrities would be lined up around the block—credit cards in hand—ready, willing, and able to pay the exorbitant price.

Lastly, let's look at the third criteria for determining value—the previous owner. According to an article on undefeated.com, a pair of previously worn Converse Fastbreaks once sold at an auction for $190,373! "Why?" you might wonder. Well, because that particular pair of Converse Fastbreaks was worn by basketball superstar Michael Jordan in the 1984 Olympics gold medal game when the United States played Spain.

Now, let's be honest. You know Jordan probably perspired in those shoes. They might've even smelled a bit. But that didn't matter to the Jordan fan who wrote the check for $190,373. That fan wanted those particular shoes because they'd once been worn and owned by basketball legend Michael Jordan.[6]

If I tried to auction off my 1987 red and white Asics cheerleading shoes, I'm pretty sure they wouldn't bring $190,373. In fact, they probably wouldn't bring $19 because they were worn an entire football and basketball season, and I'm pretty sure they have "the stank" on them. And I'm the one who owned them. Not someone famous like Jordan.

PLATINUM PROMISE

So, to recap, the value of something is determined by its rarity, the amount someone will pay for it, and its previous ownership. Well, based on those criteria, I'd say you're pretty valuable. First off, you're rare! You're one of a kind! Even if you are an identical twin, you still have your own fingerprints and unique personality that differ from your twin. Isaiah 64:8 says, "But now, O Lord, you are our Father; we are the clay, and you are our potter; we are all the work of your hand" (ESV).

God made you and me and Bethany, and He didn't use the same mold for all of us. No, He created a unique, rare masterpiece when He formed each one of us!

The second criteria that determines value is the amount someone is willing to pay for something. That also puts you in that priceless category. John 3:16 says, "For God so loved the world that He gave His only begotten Son, that whoever believes in Him should not perish but have everlasting life" (NKJV).

If you're like me, you probably memorized that verse as a young child, but have you ever really meditated on it? God gave His only Son for you! That was a high price! That was the highest price! Every time you see a cross, that should affirm just how valuable you are. The cross proves your value. Say that out loud right now, "The cross proves my value." And, I want you to say that every time you start to doubt your worth.

And, what about criteria number three that determines value? Previous ownership. First Corinthians 7:23a answers that: "You were bought at a price" (NKJV).

Or, how about 1 Peter 2:9? "But you are a chosen people, a royal priesthood, a holy nation, *God's special possession*, that you may declare the praises of him who called you out of darkness into his wonderful light" (NIV, italics added).

Romans 14:8 says, "For if we live, we live to the Lord, and if we die, we die to the Lord. So then, whether we live or whether we die, *we are the Lord's*" (ESV, italics added).

The Bible clearly says that we belong to God. If you have asked the Lord to forgive you of your sins and have given your life to Him, then you are His!

There you have it—scriptural proof that you are rare, precious, and valuable—just like platinum.

But if you don't know how much our Heavenly Father loves you, cherishes you, and values you, then you'll never walk in platinum faith. Because in order to walk in platinum faith, you have to understand that your life matters. You have to believe that no matter how you feel on any given day, that you are important to God and to His kingdom. You have to know that you were created and called for an important purpose—a platinum purpose.

I love the story of Rahab found in Joshua 2 because every time I read it, I'm encouraged that if God could use Rahab in such a mighty way, He can use me, too. Think about it. Almost every time I've ever heard someone preach about her, she's referred to as "Rahab the prostitute" or "Rahab the harlot"—almost as if that identifier were part of her actual name. You see, the world saw her as a whore, worthless, scorned, and shameful. But God looked at her through His eyes of love and saw her heart, and do you know what He saw there? He saw her faith—her platinum faith.

She would've had to have possessed platinum faith in order to do what she did. Let's read her story, beginning with Joshua 2:1:

> Then Joshua son of Nun secretly sent two spies from Shittim. "Go, look over the land," he said, "especially Jericho." So they went and entered the house of a prostitute named Rahab and stayed there.
>
> The king of Jericho was told, "Look, some of the

Israelites have come here tonight to spy out the land." So the king of Jericho sent this message to Rahab: "Bring out the men who came to you and entered your house, because they have come to spy out the whole land."

But the woman had taken the two men and hidden them. She said, "Yes, the men came to me, but I did not know where they had come from. At dusk, when it was time to close the city gate, they left. I don't know which way they went. Go after them quickly. You may catch up with them." (But she had taken them up to the roof and hidden them under the stalks of flax she had laid out on the roof.) So the men set out in pursuit of the spies on the road that leads to the fords of the Jordan, and as soon as the pursuers had gone out, the gate was shut.

Before the spies lay down for the night, she went up on the roof and said to them, "I know that the LORD has given you this land and that a great fear of you has fallen on us, so that all who live in this country are melting in fear because of you. We have heard how the LORD dried up the water of the Red Sea for you when you came out of Egypt, and what you did to Sihon and Og, the two kings of the Amorites east of the Jordan, whom you completely destroyed. When we heard of it, our hearts melted in fear and everyone's courage failed because of you, for the LORD your God is God in heaven above and on the earth below.

"Now then, please swear to me by the LORD that you will show kindness to my family, because I have shown kindness to you. Give me a sure sign that you will spare the lives of my father and mother, my brothers and sisters, and all who belong to them—and that you will save us from death."

"Our lives for your lives!" the men assured her. "If you don't tell what we are doing, we will treat you kindly and faithfully when the LORD gives us the land."

So she let them down by a rope through the window, for the house she lived in was part of the city wall. She said to them, "Go to the hills so the pursuers will not find you. Hide yourselves there three days until they return, and then go on your way." (vv. 1-16 NIV)

I find Rahab's actions so impressive. Not only did she risk her life for that of her family but she also recognized that the God of the Israelites was the One true God, and she wanted to be on His side. And, here's the thing. Rahab had no real knowledge of God or His teachings, and she hadn't experienced or seen any of the miracles she mentions, and yet she believed in Him and what He had already done and would do, without hesitation.

This couldn't have been easy for her, wheeling and dealing with these two godly spies. I'm sure she felt ashamed of her profession, and I'm sure she wondered if the two spies knew of her reputation, yet she boldly helped them, made a deal to save her life and her family's lives, and then planned their escape. That kind of courage only comes when you have platinum faith, and sister, she had it!

Of course, the story continues. Rahab makes a deal with the two spies—your lives for my life and the lives of my family. The spies agree with a few conditions. First, she is told to hang a red cord out of her window on the city wall. You see, her home was built into the city's wall—the perfect location for this plan to work. And, second, she is ordered to gather all of her family into her home because that's the only place they will be safe.

That's about all the spies gave Rahab to go on. They didn't say, "We'll return next Tuesday so be ready." In fact, they didn't give her any time frame. She simply had to believe and be ready, which she did, and she and her entire family were spared. The rest of the wall came tumbling down but not the section housing Rahab and her family. God honored her platinum faith.

In fact, did you know Rahab is only one of two women named in Hebrews 11, which is sort of the Hall of Fame for the Faithful? It's true! "By faith the prostitute Rahab, because she welcomed the spies, was not killed with those who were disobedient" (Hebrews 11:31).

Rahab the harlot ended up being a Hall of Faith-er! And what's more, she is in the direct lineage of Jesus! Rahab married an

Israelite named Salmon who was one of the spies she had hidden, and they had a son named Boaz, who grew up to be a godly man. Then, Boaz married Ruth, and they had a son, Obed. And that little boy ends up being the grandfather of King David—directly in the lineage of Jesus Christ.

That's what platinum faith will do. It'll take you out of the gutter and into the Hall of Faith chapter and make you part of the lineage of Jesus. Do you have platinum faith?

Live Brilliant: What Do You Call Yourself?

BETHANY

What sins do you attach to your name? What labels do you attach to other people's names?

My dad and I are watching *The Amazing Race*, and without fail, each team will nickname all the other teams. So far in this season, we've heard these labels: the hippies, the sisters, the blondes, the grands (as in grandpa and grandson), and the one that bothered us the most: the freaks.

Kynt and Vyxsin, aka the dating goths, aka "the freaks," were the sweetest and kindest team of the season. They quickly became fan favorites, despite the ugly nickname some of the other teams gave them.[7]

Why do we do this to each other? In a more introspective manner, why do we label ourselves?

Did you wake up this morning, look in a mirror, and have a negative thought about your appearance? I did.

Did you criticize your work today? Me, too.

Let's release this negative self-talk by replacing these labels with who God says we are, for His words are truth. Let's label ourselves this way:

Loved.

Cherished.

Precious.

PLATINUM PROJECT

Just as the spies gave Rahab two tasks to walk out in faith when they made a promise to save her and her family, there are a couple of ways you can exercise platinum faith on a daily basis.

The first?

Understand how much God loves you and truly believe it, because if you don't, you'll never walk in all that He has for you. That's why when I shared my story with you about my wonderful father at the beginning of this chapter, I said it's harder to comprehend the Heavenly Father's unconditional, all-encompassing love if you've never had anything close to that kind of love from your earthly dad. If you struggle with knowing you're loved, valued, and adored, meditate on these scriptures every day.

- "This is how God showed his love among us: He sent his one and only Son into the world that we might live through him. This is love: not that we loved God, but that he loved us and sent his Son as an atoning sacrifice for our sins" (1 John 4:9-10 NIV).

- "Even before he made the world, God loved us and chose us in Christ to be holy and without fault in his eyes. God decided in advance to adopt us into his own family by bringing us to himself through Jesus Christ. This is what he wanted to do, and it gave him great pleasure" (Ephesians 1:4-5 NLT).

- "And I am convinced that nothing can ever separate us from God's love. Neither death nor life, neither angels nor demons, neither our fears for today nor our worries about tomorrow—not even the powers of hell can separate us from God's love. No power in the sky above or in the earth below—indeed, nothing in all creation will ever be able to separate us from the love of God that is revealed in Christ Jesus our Lord" (Romans 8:38-39 NLT).

Write these scriptures on notecards then put them on your fridge or tape them to the visor in your car. Or, better yet, record yourself reading those scriptures on your smartphone, and listen to that recording over and over again until you begin to believe them! (Faith comes by hearing, right? Remember Romans 10:17.) Just know that God loves you! Listen, you couldn't earn His love, nor could you ever deserve it. None of us could. We must receive His amazing love by faith, so receive it today!

And the second way to walk in platinum faith?

Make sure you've asked Jesus to forgive your sins (see page 215 if you haven't), and then make a conscious effort to forgive yourself for your failures. You're going to have to give all of your hurts, disappointments, and rejections to God—and leave them at His feet. Instead of dwelling on what you've done wrong in your life, start meditating on the good things you've done. Start celebrating the new creation you have become because of Jesus! Start living with platinum faith, knowing that if God could use "Rahab the Harlot," He can use "Michelle the Mouthy" (if I'm being honest, that might be "my identifier") or "Serena the Sassy" or "Lucy the Liar." It doesn't matter what you've done in your past. Your Heavenly Father loves you. He thinks you're precious! He thinks you're worthy! He thinks you're a rare and special child.

DISCUSSION QUESTIONS

1. In Scripture, Rahab the prostitute risked her life to save her family but also recognized the god of the Israelites as the one true God. Because of her actions, God protected them and honored her faith. Have you ever been in a situation where you had to take someone's word about something, even though you didn't see immediate results? If so, did you start to doubt that person's word after some time? How did you respond?

2. Negative labels and self-talk focus on our sins and unflattering attributes. What are some of the negative labels you've given yourself or others? Can you see where they may have hindered a situation?

3. Trusting God is essential to walking in platinum faith. Do you understand how much God loves you, and, if so, do you truly believe it? Take some time for reflection.

CHAPTER 5

You Are Rare

BETHANY

I believe in Christianity as I believe that the sun has risen;
not only because I see it, but because by it I see every-
thing else.

C. S. Lewis

At some point in our lives, we all feel like we are unique, rare, misunderstood.

No one gets us. If only they could see our potential.

This feeling of being the underdog is why we love superhero movies so much. An ordinary kid gets bit by a spider and suddenly he has these great powers that, as the famous line goes, come with great responsibility.[1]

As we explore the platinum characteristic of being rare, we can apply it in two ways. First, we are rare because we are God's children, set apart as a royal priesthood (see 1 Peter 2:9) Second, depending fully and completely on God sounds easy but can be difficult to live out, thus we explore examples where this absolute trust and rare faith in God's provision are demonstrated.

CREATED TO PACK A PUNCH

When I was nine I rode my bike backwards down the hill behind our apartment.

Actually, it was a tiny mound of dirt, but it felt like the advanced slopes for professional skiers.

I mastered it perfectly and instructed my sister to keep her handlebars straight as she tried.

Well, she didn't listen, as per usual, bloody-skinned her elbow across the rough grates of the sidewalk concrete, and has the scar to prove it.

She cried.

I got in trouble.

My parents banished me to my room.

I didn't *force* my sister to ride her bike backwards down the hill. If she had kept her handlebars straight she wouldn't have fallen. But did my parents care about her bike-riding lack of form? No. All they cared about was that she got hurt.

The injustice was unbearable.

However, as a parent myself, I completely understand why my parents blamed me. Each time I punish my oldest son when his younger brothers get hurt, I immediately think back to this moment in fourth grade when I felt unjustly punished.

"They'll be sorry," I thought, my feet planted firmly against the white paint in a small act of defiance. "God's got special things for me and they're making me stay in my room like I did something really bad."

In that moment, I knew I could be like Sampson in the Old Testament. I could push the wall with my feet and my strength, and my righteous holy anger at the injustice of getting grounded would bring the entire three-story apartment crashing down.

As an adult, I realize how that seems to be a bit . . . mentally disturbing, if you will. Obviously I wasn't strong enough to bring down a building. Yet, as I lowered my legs from the wall, I knew two things: God was the only One who understood me, and He had a plan for me that was bigger than any parental expectation.

Looking back, though, I see that childlike faith that believed she could do anything in God's name. That rare faith that doesn't doubt for one second.

With God on my side, I was power in a small package. Created to do great things for Him. Created to pack a punch.

When Jesus talked about having faith like a mustard seed, we sometimes equate the analogy to the size of the seed. But consider, that teeny tiny seed bursts with flavor. It makes its presence known and is not to be underestimated.

We are God's children. The world feels big and scary, and

there will be times where we are misunderstood, punished, and in some cases persecuted. But we can have a huge impact on this world by letting our presence be known.

> *He said to them, "Because of your little faith. For truly, I say to you, if you have faith like a grain of mustard seed, you will say to this mountain, 'Move from here to there,' and it will move, and nothing will be impossible for you."*
> (Matthew 17:20 ESV)

Moving mountains makes our presence known.

Faith like a mustard seed.

PLATINUM PROPERTY

Platinum is one of the rarest metals, thirty times rarer than gold.[2] There are not a ton of platinum mines and the majority of them are in South Africa and Russia. Interestingly, platinum (or perhaps more accurately, metals in the platinum group of metals) has been discovered in meteorites of all things. A heavenly gift.

In fact, according to some sources, if you put all the platinum in an Olympic-sized pool, it would barely cover your ankles, but all the gold in the world could fill that same pool three times over.[3]

The rarity of platinum makes it extra special, but if you don't know what you're looking for you can end up making a costly mistake.

When something is rare it should be treasured, but the only way to know the value of something is to understand it. In the 1700s, various Spanish governments ordered platinum to be thrown into the rivers because they were afraid of platinum being mixed with gold or having platinum be used as a substitute for silver.[4]

Bye-bye platinum. You're more valuable and rarer than gold, but we don't understand what we have so we'll toss you overboard.

Walk. The. Plank.

Have you ever felt like platinum, being tossed aside because someone couldn't see your worth? How many times have you felt misunderstood? Discarded? Unimportant?

You're shining in all your brilliance and then someone comes along who doesn't recognize your value and treats you like dirt. God places a priceless value on us, and because we are His, we are set apart, His chosen.

> *You did not choose me, but I chose you and appointed you that you should go and bear fruit and that your fruit should abide, so that whatever you ask the Father in my name, he may give it to you. (John 15:16 ESV)*

And all too often, the world dismisses our values, opinions, and convictions as close-minded religious ideals. They deem us out of touch with reality and reject the truth of Scripture in our lives.

But in those moments, we hold tight to our faith and pray for those who don't understand. We ask for God to open their eyes so they can see the beauty of His love; and even more so, we ask for God to keep us humble so we can reveal more of Jesus and less of ourselves.

We also ask God to protect us, because feeling out of place and misunderstood hurts our hearts. Standing firm as a Christian can be isolating at times, which makes it that much more important to find other believers to be in fellowship with.

RARE = STATUS

Fortnite is one of the hottest video games as of this writing, with more than $3 billion in sales in 2018. The creators constantly bring out new skins (outfits and avatars) and weapons, only to have them available for a limited time.[5] Sometimes they don't release them again for over a year, and then it will only be for a one- to two-day period.

My boys are constantly talking about the skins they need and how rare they are, and they beg for money to be able to purchase the rare items for their collection. My mommy ears perk up at these requests because it means I can get some extra chores out of my boys. This also provides an opportunity to teach them the value of a dollar as they learn how quickly that dollar disappears when spent on an intangible virtual item.

Yet those rare purchases make my kids feel good about themselves.

Because having rare items means they have a higher prestige in the game.

It is a signal to other players of their status.

As I observe my kids, I realize that I do the same thing in real life.

I love slinging the nine-dollar-Salvation-Army-find authentic Coach bag across my shoulder because it makes me feel expensive *and I like that feeling.* Material items don't equate to true joy, but they definitely can bring happiness, particularly when you score a great deal.

According to *Business Insider*, studies show that we tend to value expensive items over their cheaper counterparts. "It's known as the 'marketing placebo effect.' And it doesn't just apply to things you buy for yourself, but also to things you may purchase for others—making the holidays an even more expensive time of year."[6]

We can't talk about rare items and price tags without mentioning the elusive handcrafted Birkin bag by Hermès, some of which cost up to $300,000. The demand for the bags is so high that a Birkin bag is actually an investment. Companies such as Vestiare Collective assert that the Hermès Birkin bag retains around 130 percent of its retail value at resale.[7]

Story after story pop up online from women who tried to buy or even look at a Birkin but receive a story from the salesperson about not having them in stock, an unwillingness to contact other stores or the company, and two-year-long waiting lists. The bag is hard to get, which makes it really funny when on the popular show *The Gilmore Girls*, the wealthy Emily Gilmore fawns over the Birkin bag gifted to her granddaughter Rory by her heir-to-the-Huntsberger-fortune boyfriend.

Rory comments, "Oh cool, a purse," not realizing the value she holds in her hands, which makes the point: we don't always recognize what something is worth.

More to the point, we don't always recognize what *we* are worth. The God of all creation sacrificed Himself so that we could spend eternity with Him. Yet we devalue ourselves with negative self-talk or self-harm or allow others to tear us down with their words.

Live Brilliant:
The Power of Words

MICHELLE

I was serving as a faculty member, teaching "Writing for Children" at this particular writers conference, and as I headed back to my room to drop off my laptop before dinner, I saw her.

She was walking alone, and she was sobbing.

I didn't know her that well, but she'd taken a couple of my workshops at a previous conference, and I'd had the opportunity to read a few of her stories. She was talented, and I really liked her.

When I caught up with her, I asked what was wrong, and I was horrified when she told me. Apparently, she'd just met with an editor who'd told her she wasn't a very good writer and then added, "You'll never get published."

"Discouraged" didn't even begin to describe her state of mind that night. In fact, she was ready to quit writing and leave the conference early, all because one editor was having a bad day and spoke hurtful words.

Proverbs 18:21 says the tongue holds the power of life and death. The Scriptures also say the tongue, though it is a small part of the human body, can make great boasts and cause immense damage. And, if you've ever been on the receiving end of hurtful words, like my writer friend, you know the full meaning of that scripture.

Thankfully, God gave me the opportunity to speak words of truth to her that night, convincing her she had great talent and that she needed to stay the remainder of the conference. Today, that same writer has won several awards for writing, and she just signed a multibook deal for a series of children's books.

I'm glad she didn't give up on her dream because of one editor's inaccurate and wounding words, because thousands of children all over the world are going to be ministered to through her books.

What about you? Have you let hurtful words stop you from pursuing your dreams? Or, have you let negative self-talk keep you bound in chains of low self-esteem and fear of failure? If you answered yes to either of those questions, it's time to stop replaying those hurtful words and break free from those chains that bind you.

It's time to combat negative words with God's Word. If someone says: "You are a loser," don't think on that untruth. Instead, remind yourself that God says: "You are the head and not the tail. You are an overcomer! You can do all things through Christ who gives you strength."

Put God's Word in your heart, and pretty soon, there won't be room for any words that don't line up with His Word.

PLATINUM PROMISE

Earlier in the chapter we discussed how if we have faith the size of a mustard seed, we could move mountains. I don't see a lot of peaks and cliffs relocating, but I've seen firsthand the power of God when I was in situations that seemed unmovable.

It's a rare thing to fully depend on God when He blesses us so abundantly. It's easy to fall into the trap of mistaking His goodness for our own greatness.

Financial insecurities can cause a lot of damage to us emotionally. Fear of the lights being turned off, not having enough money to buy milk, or wondering how in the world the rent is going to be paid can cloak our hearts in a darkness of doubt and depression.

The Bible says that we can trust God to provide for us. After all, does He not clothe the lilies in the valley with splendor and feed the birds of the air (see Matthew 6:26)?

The unnamed widow who gave her last coins to the offering (see Mark 12:42) and the widow of Zarephath who gave her last food to Elijah (see 1 Kings 17:7-16) proved their generosity and a faith that God would provide for them, even when they were literally at their last physical hope and resource.

These women demonstrated their faith in their willingness to give despite their dire circumstances. Their faith ranks at platinum-level for me because I tend to trust in myself . . . until I get into trouble.

To be a woman of platinum faith, I want to be like the few, the misunderstood, the rare women in Scripture who believed in God so much they were willing to do anything and willing to give everything.

WHEN FAITH TAKES A NOSEDIVE

My faith was tested when Justin and I got married. Justin was a youth minister, and after we got pregnant with our first son, I quit my job to be a stay-at-home mom. We moved from the

Orlando area to right outside of Tampa in an apartment complex that cost half of Justin's monthly take-home salary. Not the wisest financial decision.

For the first time, we really felt the loss of my income as our expenses went up and the money didn't stretch anymore. Add to it postpartum depression that lasted for eighteen months, in which I'm thoroughly ashamed to admit that the bills got so overwhelming that avoidance became my choice and envelope after envelope remained unopened.

My faith took a nosedive as I emotionally withdrew from everyone.

The fastest way to bury yourself in debt is pretend like it doesn't exist. We felt beaten and bruised, and it was the toughest time of our marriage. Poor Justin didn't know what to do with me and I didn't know what to do with myself. But God is good and things got better.

Over the next nine years, Justin was given a few raises, we had two more babies, and we reached a place where we knew how much we could spend on extras. Our health insurance was great until the new presidential policies took effect, but still, we managed.

Then the day came that we'd dreaded for years.

The short story is this: the church leadership was in transition. We were asked to get on board or get out.

Unable to ride that sinking ship, we got out.

And thus started the hardest year of our lives: financially, emotionally, and definitely spiritually.

Our faith gets tested in the low times. I didn't want to go to church or be around church people. I didn't know how to help my husband bear the "household provider" burden he carried without putting our little boys into full-time daycare, which, after much research, I discovered would take the majority of any take-home pay I'd receive if I started working again. My résumé now consisted of a several-year gap of sparse unemployment, and

I didn't think that companies would give much weight with my experience working side-by-side with Justin in our youth ministry, coaching cheerleading at the local high school, and writing a couple of books.

And honestly, deep in my heart, I felt like God was telling me *not* to go get a job, but instead, I felt the weight of His presence and peace about staying home. And Justin agreed.

But we had to make money.

Justin worked his guts out while we waited for a military seat to open up so he could start working full time with the National Guard; but in the interim, he got an entry-level position at a company, delivered pizza after work, worked at Chick-fil-A for a hot minute, and went to night classes to get an IT certification he knew he'd need.

At the same time, I homeschooled the boys, went back to school to finish out the three undergraduate classes that I needed so I could graduate, started Serious Writer Academy, and took on as many freelance writing projects as I could.

And God provided work at *just the right times.*

A penny not spent is a penny saved, so along with hustling, my mission was to get our monthly expenses as low as possible. Rice with fried eggs on top became one of my favorite meals at this time, and the occasional tacos from Tijuana Tuesdaze specials were like Thanksgiving. We ate a lot of cereal and blue-box macaroni and cheese.

And we survived.

But spiritually, it took a lot longer. We weren't mad at God— in fact, we trusted in Him more than we ever had before because we were literally depending on Him for our daily bread. My faith stretched as I learned to rely on God for things that I'd always taken for granted before. Out of all my years of being a Christian, I realized that this type of dependency on God for our needs was rare and that I'd misunderstood what true faith was.

FAITH FOR PROVISION

Ruth and Naomi demonstrated a rare faith, too. Neither woman had a husband to care for them, so Ruth took to gleaning the harvest fields. In those days, the edges of the harvest were left for the poor to gather so they could have a meal for their own tables. In fact, it was a God-given directive:

> *When you reap the harvest of your land, you shall not reap your field right up to its edge, neither shall you gather the gleanings after your harvest. And you shall not strip your vineyard bare, neither shall you gather the fallen grapes of your vineyard. You shall leave them for the poor and for the sojourner: I am the Lord your God.*
>
> *(Leviticus 19:9-10 ESV)*

Ruth was a Moabite, which, along with poverty, qualified her to glean from the fields, and so she walked the edges of the field taking what was needed for her and Naomi. It was not a safe situation for a woman to be working in those fields, but work she did. And as she worked, God provided more than food for their table.

Our Heavenly Father gave them security and protection in the form of Boaz, a relative of Naomi's deceased husband. "Because of his relationship with Elimelech, Boaz was actually a 'ga'al,' or kinsman-redeemer—a man required to take care of the widows of his kin people and who was responsible for marrying a childless widow and having a child with her so that the names of each Jewish man would continue. (This is called 'levirate marriage.' See Deuteronomy 25:5, 6)."[8]

God led Ruth and Naomi back into community. To His people.

And having a platinum faith means that we allow God to shepherd us back into community as well, even when it hurts and even when it's hard. There is safety in having the protection of other believers on your side.

PLATINUM PROJECT

Maybe you've been through this fight, too. If you've ever watched a payment deadline go by because the choice was to either pay Discover or put gas in the car, you know what it's like to feel out of control and helpless. You know how it feels to be completely reliant on God for each and every cent, for blessings that often go unappreciated and taken for granted.

Maybe you've felt helpless, unimportant. Maybe you've felt lonely standing on the promises of God and it seems the world is passing you by without a second glance.

Maybe you've felt misunderstood.

But beloved, you are a daughter of the One true King, and as all fairytales imply, being a princess is a rare thing. You are rare because you have been chosen. You are His. And if you find yourself in a situation that seems hopeless, remember the mustard seed with the rare faith to move mountains, stand on the Word of God, and make your presence as a Daughter of the King known.

DISCUSSION QUESTIONS

1. The author shares three stories in Scripture where women demonstrated platinum faith for God's provision. An unnamed widow gave her last coin to the offering and Zarephath's widow gave her last food to Elijah. Ruth and Naomi's platinum faith allowed God to shepherd them back into community. Also, the author mentioned she tended to trust herself when it came to finances until she got into trouble. Which of these examples can you best identify with and why?

2. We read about a young writer who let an editor's words discourage her. Because she was encouraged by someone else, she became a successful author. Have you ever let hurtful words stop you from pursuing your dreams? Or have you let negative self-talk keep you bound in chains of low self-esteem and fear of failure? If so, what was your most common negative self-talk? Where and when do you think you picked this up?

3. Think of a time when you felt lonely standing on God's promises. How did He move in the situation?

CHAPTER 6

Your Faith Shines Brightly

MICHELLE

*We are indeed the light of the world but only if our switch
is turned on.*

John Hagee

When you were a child, did you ever sing the song "This Little Light of Mine"? We used to sing it at vacation Bible school, and sometimes I still find myself singing those simple, yet powerful lyrics: "This little light of mine. I'm gonna let it shine. Let it shine. Let it shine. Shine. Shine."

Of course, that's easier sang than done—especially in today's world. In recent days, if you let your light shine too brightly, you're liable to get attacked by those who aren't on this same journey of faith. But that doesn't mean we should hide our individual and collective lights under a bushel so that we don't offend others. It just means we should let our lights shine without a judgmental filter.

Matthew 5:16 says, "Let your light shine before others, that they may see your good deeds and glorify your Father in heaven" (NIV). Notice that verse *doesn't* say, "Let your light shine on others and expose all of their wrongdoings so that you can tell them how messed up they are."

Letting your light shine means allowing your inner joy— your faith—to ooze out of your every pore, so much so, that you don't have to "preach" at others to follow Jesus. Your quiet, yet effective, witness will cause the people you encounter to *want* to know your Jesus. People don't respond positively to that attacking, judgmental approach. The Word says it's the love of God that draws men unto Him (Romans 2:4), not the meanness of overzealous Christians. I saw this truth played out firsthand when I took my two teenage daughters and their best friends to Florida for spring break one year.

On the very first day of our vacay, we grabbed our sunscreen, magazines, towels, beach chairs, sunglasses, and water bottles and headed for the sandy white beach. As we strolled down the boardwalk in search of the perfect spot to stake our claim, I noticed a group of men and women who were obviously not dressed for the beach. The men wore long pants and long-sleeved shirts and ties, and the women wore long dark skirts and long-sleeved white blouses. I wondered what they were doing there.

I didn't have to wonder long.

"Repent, you prostitutes, dressed in your bikini bathing suits!" one of the men yelled through a bullhorn.

I glanced down at my bathing suit and my girls' bathing suits, and I immediately went into the "Oh no he didn't" mode.

"Turn from your wicked ways, you heathens," he continued his rant. "Or you will burn in hell!"

Abby, who was a senior in high school at the time, looked at the man with the bullhorn in disbelief and said, "Mom, say something! He is making Christians look so bad!"

Ab has always been a bit of a spitfire, but she was right. He WAS making Christians look bad, and he wasn't accomplishing anything for the kingdom of God.

Finally, I couldn't take it anymore.

"Sir, can I speak with you a moment?"

He completely ignored me.

"Listen," I continued, as he turned his back to me, "I am also a Christian. And though I admire your tenacity for reaching the lost, I'm thinking there might be a better way to accomplish that."

Still, he ignored me and continued calling girls who passed by "prostitutes" and "Jezebels."

"Sir, please stop with the name-calling," I urged, as he walked away from me.

One of the women handed me a tract, as we headed toward

the beach. He didn't want to hear what I had to say, and the feeling was mutual. As Abby and I walked back to join our little spring break group, he pointed the bullhorn right at us and shouted, "Prostitutes!"

I grabbed Abby's hand, afraid she might go back and tell him what he could do with his bullhorn, and we moved to the far end of the beach so we wouldn't have to hear the ugliness anymore.

The whole encounter left me so sad inside.

That group of men and women were very committed to their cause, working all day in the hot sun every day we were there, yet what did they accomplish? They simply alienated everyone within the sound of their bullhorns. No one cared what they had to say. No one wanted to read their tracts.

You know, someone once said people don't care how much you know until they know how much you care. See, it didn't matter that these folks could rattle off Bible verses, one right after another, because no one "heard" them. We all tuned them out.

PLATINUM PROMISE

They were not a good or accurate representation of our Lord. Jesus didn't shout "Prostitute!" when he encountered the woman at the well, the woman who had already been married five times and was living with another man. Instead, He offered her living water, a new start, a refreshing for her spirit. In fact, Jesus always led with love when He encountered sinners. Remember the story of the woman who used her tears and her hair to wash the feet of Jesus?

> *When one of the Pharisees invited Jesus to have dinner with him, he went to the Pharisee's house and reclined at the table. A woman in that town who lived a sinful life learned that Jesus was eating at the Pharisee's house, so she came there with an alabaster jar of perfume. As she stood behind him at his feet weeping, she began to wet his feet with her tears. Then she wiped them with her hair, kissed them and poured perfume on them.*

> When the Pharisee who had invited him saw this,
> he said to himself, "If this man were a prophet, he would
> know who is touching him and what kind of woman she
> is—that she is a sinner."
>
> Jesus answered him, "Simon, I have something to
> tell you."
>
> "Tell me, teacher," he said.
>
> "Two people owed money to a certain moneylender.
> One owed him five hundred denarii, and the other fifty.
> Neither of them had the money to pay him back, so he
> forgave the debts of both. Now which of them will love
> him more?"
>
> Simon replied, "I suppose the one who had the bigger
> debt forgiven."
>
> "You have judged correctly," Jesus said.
>
> Then he turned toward the woman and said to
> Simon, "Do you see this woman? I came into your house.
> You did not give me any water for my feet, but she wet
> my feet with her tears and wiped them with her hair. You
> did not give me a kiss, but this woman, from the time I
> entered, has not stopped kissing my feet. You did not put
> oil on my head, but she has poured perfume on my feet.
> Therefore, I tell you, her many sins have been forgiven—
> as her great love has shown. But whoever has been forgiven
> little loves little."
>
> Then Jesus said to her, "Your sins are forgiven."
>
> The other guests began to say among themselves,
> "Who is this who even forgives sins?" .
>
> Jesus said to the woman, "Your faith has saved you;
> go in peace." (Luke 7:36-50 NIV)

See, we can be a light in this world without condemning those who are still searching for God. The spiritual leaders of the day condemned this woman. They were appalled at her actions. But Jesus showed her mercy. He saw her heart and loved her.

One of the spiritual giants in my life once said, "It's not your job to fix everybody. If you'll just let your light shine and represent God in a great way, people will be drawn to the God in you.

Your life becomes more effective than any sermon you could ever preach at them."

Bottom line, we don't have to be the Holy Ghost sheriff. God doesn't need us to tell others where they are messing up in life. (Trust me, they already know.) He just needs us to let our lights shine. He needs us to be so full of His love that it spills out onto everyone we encounter.

LET YOUR LIGHT SHINE—NO MATTER WHAT!

That means we should let our lights shine even in the midst of difficult people. I know that's not an easy thing to do but think of it this way—it's probably not about you. God may have strategically positioned you so He can shine brightly through you onto those who might not encounter Him any other way.

Maybe God is using you as the only Christian—the only light—in their world. When you look at it that way, it makes it easier to endure. That's what happened to a good friend of mine. She was feeling very victimized at work. Being the lone Christian in her workplace, she was often left out of conversations, rarely invited to lunch, and sometimes referred to as "that Christian girl." It was really hard for her. She often ate lunch in her car, listening to encouraging podcasts, just so she could go back into work and finish the day.

Her direct boss was very good at his job, and she was excited that he was training her because she knew it was a great opportunity for her to grow in her skill set. There was only one problem: he hated her guts. Or at least, that's what she thought. He went out of his way to be mean to her. Still, my friend kept being respectful, trying her hardest, and letting her light shine. After about ten months, she was promoted and transferred to a different city. On her last day at that location, two of her coworkers left early, which meant my friend had to finish her work and their work before turning in her key and leaving—for good. As she was finishing up, her direct boss thanked her for her hard work and wished her good luck at her next post.

But that's not all.

Nervously, he said, "You know, I tried not to like you, but you're just so likeable. You're not like any other religious person I've ever met."

My friend laughed and answered, "Thank you, I think."

Then the two of them talked for another forty-five minutes as he shared how he had been really hurt by his father who was a pastor. She was able to comfort him and tell him that his Heavenly Father loved him and approved of him, even if his earthly father hadn't.

As she walked to her car that night, she called me and shared what had transpired. We rejoiced together over God's plan that is so much bigger than any one person. I truly believe God positioned my precious friend in that hostile work environment for that one man, her boss, who needed to know that not all Christians were judgmental and mean, and so she could tell him that his Heavenly Father loved him unconditionally.

When we are willing to shine for Jesus, even if that means enduring some discomfort or even persecution, we are walking in platinum faith.

PLATINUM PROPERTY

At first glance, you might not be able to determine which is silver and which is platinum because both are cool metals with gray undertones. But, upon closer inspection, you can usually distinguish between the two because platinum is much brighter and shinier. Even platinum pieces that haven't been cleaned in a long time maintain their luster better than silver pieces that must be polished often because they tarnish so easily.

Though platinum doesn't tarnish as heavily or as quickly as silver, its surface can become rather dull over time.

Sort of like our platinum faith.

One day, you can be standing on the promises, praising the Lord, and shouting the hallelujahs, but when your breakthrough doesn't happen as quickly as you'd hoped, your platinum faith can become cloudy at best. And, it can happen so slowly and sneakily, a little less luster every day, that when you wake up one day and your platinum faith no longer has its shine, you may not have any idea how it happened or when it happened.

I walked through this with my sister, Martie, as we cared for our mama before she went to heaven. Mom had been diagnosed with terminal cancer, and though she was more than ready to go home and be with Jesus and our father who had passed two years before, we weren't ready. The doctors had done everything they could do for Mom, so hospice was called in to make her comfortable. Martie and I met with her main doctor and the hospice workers, and we prayerfully decided to do everything in our power to keep Mom at my sister's house instead of a twenty-four-hour nursing care facility.

So, that's what we did.

It was our greatest privilege to care for our wonderful mother, but it was also one of the most difficult seasons of our lives. Every single day we fought discouragement, sadness, hopelessness, and fatigue. It was a journey we never wanted to take—a role reversal we never asked for—but a calling we were more than willing to answer.

Maybe you're in the same situation or you know someone who is. More than likely, you fall into one of these categories because approximately 22.4 million households currently provide physical and emotional assistance to friends and relatives age fifty and older, according to the National Alliance of Caregiving.[1]

It's a reality.

And, as caregivers you often feel isolated from the world and overwhelmed with the reality of what's actually going on—that is, your loved one is ill, and oftentimes, the prognosis is not good.

Just those two things alone could dull your platinum faith's luster but add to them the constant stress and fatigue that accompanies caregiving, and your platinum faith might be luster-less.

That's where my sister and I found ourselves after several months of sitting with our mom, performing wound care, changing her colostomy bag, and all of the many other tasks we had mastered in order to provide the best care for our sweet mama. Martie and I would take turns at Mom's side so the other one could go for a walk, get an ice cream cone, get our nails done, or run needed errands. Many times when I had a few hours away, I'd park my SUV at one of my favorite scenic spots in Lawrence County, Indiana, and I'd put Keith Moore's CD in and play "Thank You Lord for the Holy Ghost" over and over again.

As I looked out over the beautiful countryside—sometimes through tears—and listened to those powerful lyrics, I would feel my luster returning.

Just like platinum jewelry comes back to life after soaking it in warm soapy water, immersing myself in God's presence restored my platinum faith, and I was ready to face another day.

It's not that we've lost our faith when we lose our luster; it's just that we're often weary in the well-doing. Maybe that's why Galatians 6:9 encourages, "Let us not become weary in doing good, for at the proper time we will reap a harvest if we do not give up" (NIV).

We can't give up. We have to stay in the fight—the good fight of faith (1 Timothy 6:12)—no matter how long the battle rages on. Fight on, my sister, fight on!

Even if your platinum faith is a little lackluster today, the very fact that you're taking time to read this book reveals your desire for restoration, and God will honor your faithful heart.

Live Brilliant:
Keep the Light Shining

BETHANY

"Brothers, if anyone is caught in any transgression, you who are spiritual should restore him in a spirit of gentleness. Keep watch on yourself, lest you too be tempted. Bear one another's burdens, and so fulfill the law of Christ." (Galatians 6:1-2 ESV)

When we see our sisters in Christ struggling with a sin, the Bible says we are to gently restore and bear their burdens. We are to be a light shining for them as they wade through the darkness. Too many times, however, we pour lighter fluid on our flames and end up burning the relationship in our zeal to "help her see the light."

Girlfriends, we have to know when and how to be that light.

Sometimes God calls you *to be* the person to help your friend through a rough patch.

Sometimes God calls you *to pray* for the person who can help your friend.

When my sister was separated from her husband, I tried desperately to be the light for her. She had met a guy online who filled her ears with sweet words, and slowly she grew apart from her spouse.

My sister was hurting, depressed, and desperately

wanted to feel loved, so she found it in the safety of someone who was physically too far away to hurt her, but emotionally available at the ping of a text.

I pulled the "Big Sister" card, the Christian card, the "You're going to make a huge mistake," card, the "I'm always here for you no matter what" card, but nothing worked.

My mom was saying the same things, so my sister was getting two earfuls of words she didn't want to hear.

As her sister, I felt like I had permission to speak truth into her life in a way that many wouldn't be able to. Galatians 6:1 tells us to help restore those who are caught in sin, but despite my attempts to convince her she was walking a dangerous path, it was our relationship that fractured.

I became the enemy instead of the ally.

I didn't know what to do so I started praying that God would send someone she *would* listen to and, more specifically, that God would intervene *and interfere* in her affair with the other man.

As the affair went on, I watched some of my sister's friends berate her, belittle her, and unfriend her from social media. She became more detached. I knew that even though I adamantly disagreed with what was happening in her life, I had to make it clear to my sister that I would always be there.

How could I be a light to her if I shunned her or disowned her?

Romans 15:1 says that we who are strong ought to bear with the failings of the weak, and not to please ourselves (NIV). Abandoning someone in their time of need isn't bearing with failings. It's letting someone swim into the deep end of shark-infested waters while we sit in safety on the boat.

You may not be the person who God uses to pull a friend back to protection, but how much love is there for each other if we don't toss multiple floaties for them to grab onto?

Throw the life preserver.

Through God's power and mercy, my sister was able to restore her marriage, and honestly, you'd never know there had ever been this type of betrayal. She and her husband are more in love than ever, with a deeper trust built on top of what they've overcome.

We have to keep the light shining and always, always, always leave space in our hearts for our loved ones to find their way back.

PLATINUM PROJECT

When I inherited some platinum pieces of jewelry from my late mother-in-law, I researched how to care for them, and I discovered that dulling prevention is way easier than treating existing dulling and tarnishing. So, if I'm going to apply hand lotion or spray perfume or hairspray, I always remove any platinum jewelry I might be wearing to avoid getting any dulling residue on them. And, after wearing them, before storing them, I simply wipe them down with a special jewelry cloth until they shine like new once again.

I think these are good practices to follow when it comes to our platinum faith, as well. Daily faith maintenance is key—key to preventing the dulling of our faith. In the same way I protect my platinum jewelry from residue, we should protect our platinum faith from things that might cloud it, such as: saying things that aren't in line with God's Word or hanging out regularly with people who don't believe in God or His faithfulness. And, just like my platinum pieces need a daily wipe down, we need a daily cleansing from our Heavenly Father. We need time in His Word, letting it wash over us. As we study the Bible, our minds are renewed into the very mind of Christ, according to Romans 12:2 and Ephesians 4:23.

So, that's your platinum project—that is, guard your heart and your faith from negative outside influences and get into the routine of washing yourself in the Word of God every single day. That will restore luster to your platinum faith, and you'll be able to let your light shine in such a powerful way that people will be drawn to God just by being in your presence.

DISCUSSION QUESTIONS

1. In the narrative, Michelle gives an example of Christians shouting negative, judgmental remarks toward her daughters when they were on a family vacation. How might their accusations have affected other Christians? How might they have affected non-Christians?

2. When we see our sisters in Christ struggling with a sin, the Bible says we are to gently restore and bear their burdens. Reflect on a time when you or a loved one struggled and how you approached the situation. Was the situation approached with judgment or love?

3. Daily faith maintenance prevents our faith from becoming dull. What are some practical steps you can take to guard your heart and faith from negative outside influences?

CHAPTER 7

You Were Created to Bond

BETHANY

Friendship is born at that moment when one person says to another: "What! You too? I thought I was the only one."

C. S. Lewis

I was a lonely child. The term *introvert* wasn't widely used, so I was simply quiet, shy, and reserved. People liked me but didn't really include me in their list of friends. Invitations to sleepovers and parties were nonexistent, so I clung to my youth-group relationships and made friends with the characters in books.

And yes, it may have been just as pitiful as it sounds.

Switching schools between the seventh- and eighth-grade years seemed like a good idea. Knowing people before transitioning to high school makes sense. Unless you're a shy, reserved girl who doesn't have the confidence to put herself out there.

That year my class went on a science theme park field trip, and we were required to be in groups of four. Afraid that I'd be placed in a group with strangers, I sought out Holly, the one girl who was in a few of my classes and stood near her, as she stood with her two best friends. By angling my body toward them, no one else came over to our little cluster, and I successfully secured a spot in a group.

I'm not sure the other girls were happy to have me hanging around, but I did my best to not annoy them. When they wanted to go into a shop, I went in, too, pretending to browse items I didn't care about and definitely couldn't afford.

Our class was required to check in at the planetarium as the grand finale. Once we arrived, my group was no longer obliged to have me as their tagalong. I followed the girls to the front row where they found some empty seats, and I parked myself at the end of their group, with empty seats to my left until another group of girls snagged them. Sitting alone in the dim theater waiting for the constellations video to begin was incredibly awkward. Chatter and laughter echoed in the metal room while I found myself leaning a little to the left for a few minutes and then shifting a little to the right so both groups of girls on either side of me would think that I was with the other group.

Looking back, I wish cell phones had been invented so I could have had something to do and a way to connect with someone— anyone—but reality was, I was truly and completely alone.

And yet, age brings clarity. The older I get, the more confident I become in who I am instead of the impression I want others to have of me. Comfort trumps cuteness, although when I was younger I swore never to be someone who chose the sensible shoe over the stylish one. Yet here I am, mother of three, trekking outside in Sketcher's walking shoes without a care in the world who notices.

That shallow way of thinking didn't transform because I grew up but because of who I grew into.

The young girl who spent so much time alone *and* worried that others would notice she was alone has bloomed into a woman who found her confidence in what God thought of her. One universal truth is this: the older we get, the more we realize what we don't know, and I know that even though I've grown in being comfortable with who I am and Whose I am, there is still a lot of path to cover and a lot of growing up to be done.

My heart goes out to all the kids who feel lonely on field trips or out of place because they're awkward around people. I tell my sons to keep an eye out for kids who seem to be loners or kids who look like they might need a friend because back in the day, that loner kid was me.

As an adult, I recognize that my introverted tendencies didn't help when it came to making friends easily, but I believe regardless of whether or not it's easy to connect with others, we are called to love others because we love God. And He created us to connect.

Striving for platinum faith means staying open and communicative to others and God.

So, let's explore this platinum characteristic of being created to bond.

PLATINUM PROPERTY

Platinum is a transition metal, which means it bonds easily with other elements. It's not a *loner* metal. This ability to "be friends" with other elements makes platinum a valuable commodity.

As believers, we want to attract others to us, to spread the joy of Jesus and the message of hope and salvation. We want to have a strong connection with the people around us, to feel included in the group. But sometimes we're the outsiders. How do we determine the proper amount of relationship-building to ensure that we're following Jesus's command to love our neighbors?

At one point in time, I'd argue that you couldn't be a loner and spread the Word of God; and that monks who hid away in monasteries weren't really helping evangelize at all. But with social media and the internet, I can't get away with saying that anymore. In fact, with the expansion of online communication and grocery delivery, my goal of never having to leave the house could actually happen.

Instead, the argument becomes more spiritual, more relative to how God created us.

We aren't meant to be by ourselves.

If you think about, is God even meant to be alone?

Genesis 1:1 says that in the beginning, *God* created the heavens and the earth, but the word for *God* used there is not the singular form. In what is truly a fascinating word study, *Elohim* is both used singularly and in the plurality, and in this case, many

theologians agree that God is referring to Himself as the Trinity.[1]
God. In three Persons. At the beginning of time. Together.
Then He created the angels to be with Him.

And then He created *us* with the purpose of true, deep, and meaningful relationship.

Sin destroyed that, and the separation that followed is in the process of being repaired until the day Jesus comes back to take God's children home. To be together. For eternity.

Our faith suffers when we cut ourselves off from spending time with people, but most importantly from other believers. If your faith is the most important part of who you are and how you identify yourself, then someone who doesn't understand that most important part of you can never fully understand *you*.

It wasn't good for man to be alone despite the vast amount of animals he was in charge of. Shortly after breathing life into dust, God created Adam's partner out of his rib because Adam needed someone who would understand the most important part of his soul (see Genesis 2:18).

Connection breeds intimacy, and the smaller our circle, the more vulnerable we allow ourselves to become. We open up. We share. We relate and empathize, and suddenly someone makes a statement that you thought only you were crazy enough to think but never brave enough to say out loud and an instantaneous friendship is born.

The older I get, the smaller my circle of friends gets. However, the relationships go deeper and I feel safe enough to truly be myself.

PERSONALITY TYPING

The metal platinum bonds easily with other metals. It can take work to build our people skills to a point where we can bond easily with others. This did not come naturally to me. It wasn't until I was working in direct sales that I learned some skills for being able to connect with people quickly and authentically. From a sales perspective, it's important to have people like you so they'll purchase from you. From a faith perspective, it's important to connect with people so that God can use you for His purpose.

Using the popular DISC personality profile, you can break down a woman's personality by simple cues. Is her jewelry colorful, bold, or simple? Is she soft-spoken or authoritative? This test has been the most helpful personality identifier I've come across. In fact, we utilize it within our company so that we can all work best with each other according to our strengths and helping in our weaknesses.

The quickest and easiest way to determine someone's DISC personality is to pay attention to how he or she answers the question-statement, "Tell me about yourself."

A high-D (dominant) personality may share her achievements and accomplishments.

A high-I (influential) personality may share about her activities and the organizations she's involved in.

A high-S (steady) personality may share about her family.

A high-C (conscientious) personality may respond by asking what exactly you want to know. Do you want to know about her family? her job? her hobbies? She needs more information to answer you properly.

Similarly, mirroring the personality of your companion will help her feel at ease. Speaking at a measured and softer pace will make the high-S personality feel comfortable. Conversely, talking excitedly fast will annoy the high-C personality but will endear you to the high-I. With a high-D, get straight to the point.

You get the picture.

When I was a youth minister's wife, I felt that it was my duty to greet and connect with the adult members of the congregation. On Wednesday evenings during the church family meal, I often would make rounds to the tables to say hi and give hugs, and Sunday mornings were full of "So great to see you!" welcomes.

The more I mirrored their greeting, the more comfortable they became around me.

And isn't that the point?

I am not the most important person in the room.

My comfort is not the priority.

"'The great problem in sales is that we all tend to see the world through our own eyes,' says Brian Tracy of Solana Beach, California, a bestselling author of more than 50 books and 500 audio and video programs on sales, leadership and business success, including *The Psychology of Selling*. 'As a result, we tend to treat everybody else as if they are the way we are.'"[2]

So I learned to mirror and to quickly gauge a personality profile by the way someone walked, held their head, chose their jewelry and accessories, and spoke. In fact, my life verse says to consider others more highly than myself, not looking to my own interests, but the *interests of others* (see Philippians 2:3-4 NIV).

By clinging to this platinum property and applying it to a platinum faith, we see that bonding easily with others allows us to engage in deeper relationships. It helps break down walls. It makes the other person feel comfortable, perhaps comfortable enough to share the raw and vulnerable and ugly parts that they need to pull into the light instead of hide in the darkness.

When we feel like no one understands us, we can believe the lie that no one truly does.

Some may argue that this is disingenuous, that by mirroring personalities we are not showing our true selves. To a certain extent, I'd agree. Personality mirroring is a helpful technique to help others feel at ease, but you also have to be real and transparent if you want to have a deeper relationship.

We all have times when we feel dominant, or steady, or influential, or conscientious. Our "resting personality" may be really high in one of those categories, but that doesn't mean we are void of the others. "Personality theory is predicated on the belief that individuals will demonstrate more often than not a distinct style with definite behaviors and preferences as identified using the DISC profile than the average person."[3]

Think about the people who make you feel most comfortable. They may be your complete opposite but something about them is familiar. Married couples often mirror each other without realizing it because they're so in tune.

When we don't have someone who shows interest in us, we can feel quite alone.

It's why we can feel lonely in a crowded room.

Growing in platinum faith means stepping out of our comfort zone and learning the skill of bonding with others.

PLATINUM PROMISE

Growing our faith doesn't happen by accident.

Similar to how we must bond with people, we must absolutely take the time to create an intimate relationship with God. After we take a good long thorough self-evaluation, all too often busyness interferes with communication with God, and that's not having a platinum-level faith.

Remember Daniel, who prayed at his window three times a day, even when threatened that doing so could end his life (and it very nearly did!) (see Daniel 6:10-28 ESV). The level of faith to defy the law of the day is astounding.

I wonder if Daniel was frightened—I mean, he easily could have said, "Well, I have to follow the law of the land," and just prayed three times a day behind closed doors. But instead, his desire to commune with God was stronger than the law, and in defiance of the king's order, Daniel prayed in full view.

Is my communication with God that strong? Would I have the courage to resist the temptation to pray in secret? Would you?

Even though we don't live in a country where the laws are that extreme, in what areas does my faith have a lack of that platinum quality of being transitional? Not a loner? Communicative?

Isn't it true that we need to stay open and allow communication not only to other people, but also to God?

When King Nebuchadnezzar needed his dream interpreted, it was because of Daniel's relationship with God that the dream's meaning was revealed. Daniel was so in tune with God that the king recognized God's spirit inside of him (see Daniel 4:9). And it was this incredible relationship with God that had a residual effect across the kingdom. King Darius prayed for Daniel's God to save him when Daniel was thrown into the lion's den.

The king, who made the edict against praying to Daniel's God, *prayed to Daniel's God.*

Ironic.

Wonderful.

And platinum.

Live Brilliant: Your Platinum Project

MICHELLE

Abigail Adams once said, "Learning is not attained by chance, it must be sought for with ardor and diligence."

Life is busy.

I get it, but if we don't make time for God and His Word, we'll never walk in all that He has for us. We'll never accomplish all that He has for us to do. Bottom line, we'll never have platinum faith if we don't spend time in His Word and at His feet.

If you have a significant other, do you remember when you first fell in love? Every minute apart seemed like an eternity! You couldn't wait until the next time you could be together. You thought about him all the time. You talked about him all the time. Everything reminded you of him. Just hearing his name made you smile. Well, that's how we should feel about Jesus! After all, He is our first love, yet it's easy to lose sight of that fact in the busyness of everyday life.

So how do you fall back in love with Jesus? Spend time in His presence. The more time you spend with Jesus, the more time you'll want to spend with Him. Having your devotional/prayer time shouldn't feel like an obligation, but I know sometimes it can become just another item on our "to do" list that we check off after completing the task. I find that getting a good devotional book helps me stay committed to reading God's Word and meditating on His promises. Trust me, a good devotional can make all the difference. Suzanne Hadley Gosselin, an author friend of mine who follows me on social media, learned that both of my daughters were expecting babies and was thoughtful enough to send them her new devotional just for moms called *Grit and Grace: Devotions for Warrior Moms* (Harvest House). My oldest daughter, Abby, told me just this week: "I love that devotional so much. Her writing ministers to me right where I'm at—in the middle of raising two little ones. I look forward to it every morning." So, find a devotional that speaks to you and you'll start looking forward to your private time with God, too!

And, here's the best part. The God of this universe, the Great I Am, the King of Kings, is looking forward to spending time with you! He can't wait to reveal things to you in His Word. He adores you, and He has been waiting for you. In fact, God created us because He wanted to be with us. In his book *Hearing God: Developing a Conversational Relationship with God*, Dallas Willard writes: "God has created us for intimate friendship with himself, both now and forever."[4]

How awesome is that? So, take time to study the Bible today. Don't feel like you have to read four chapters every morning. Don't let guilt and condemnation overtake you because you only read three verses yesterday. Sometimes, you may only want to read a few verses and mediate on that short passage of scripture. Other days, you may read several chapters in one sitting. There's no right or wrong way to get into His Word. You might even want to make the most of your commute time and listen to an audio version of the Bible. Are you so excited about spending more time with God and studying His Word?

There are so many benefits to reading the Bible and giving it first priority in your life. Here are just a few of the benefits listed in Proverbs 2–3.

You'll gain:

- Knowledge of God
- Wisdom
- Understanding
- Good sense
- Know-how to find the right course of action every time
- Discernment
- Joy
- Wise planning
- Direction for our paths

So, go ahead. Dive into God's Word today. If you would like a "read the Bible through in a year" program or other Bible reading plans, here are a few resources for you:

- www.biblestudytools.com/bible-reading-plan/
- https://itunes.apple.com/us/app/bible-in-one-year/id504133402?mt=8 (Free app)
- www.biblegateway.com/reading-plans/?version=NIV

Once you put God and His Word first place in your life, you'll become closer and you'll long to be closer still. You'll bond with God in a way you hadn't dreamed possible. And, just like that old hymn says, you'll be one in the bond of love and you'll have joined your spirit with the Spirit of God. Amen.

DISCUSSION QUESTIONS

1. In Scripture, Daniel prayed at his window three times a day, even when threatened that doing so could end his life. His desire to commune with God was stronger than his fear of the law. Is your communication level with God as strong as Daniel's? If not, how would you describe your communication level with God?

2. Do you make an effort to bond with others or do you guard yourself emotionally?

3. What are some practical steps you can take to overcome busyness and put God and His Word first in your life?

Chapter 8

You Are Malleable in the Father's Hands

Michelle

You see, a potter can only mold the clay when it lies completely in his hand. It requires complete surrender.

Corrie Ten Boom

As I sat waiting for the meeting, my six picture-book manuscripts neatly stacked atop my planner, I smiled. It was finally happening. People were taking notice of my writing. I would soon be a published children's book author.

The meeting began, and my boss hurried through the other items on the agenda. Finally, it was my turn. We were going to discuss *my* manuscripts. I fidgeted in my seat with excitement.

"Michelle, in order to give your books a better chance of selling, we have decided to put our children's minister's name on the front cover," my boss explained to the room full of people. "She already has quite a following, and her name recognition alone will guarantee sales."

My mouth dropped open. My heart sank. And, my eyes filled with tears.

"You mean, my name isn't going to be on the books at all?" I asked, trying to remain calm. "But I wrote the books! I didn't even discuss them with her."

"Yes, but you work for us, and you wrote the books on company time," she said, sternly. "And, we've decided that this is the best way to proceed."

All eyes fixed on me.

My eyes, which I thought were fixed on Jesus, were suddenly fixed on my manuscripts and myself.

I got up, grabbed my stories, and left the meeting without saying a word.

That night, after I relayed the whole fiasco to my husband, he consoled me as only a husband can do, and then he said, "Why don't you just give them the books? They aren't yours anyway. They're God's."

Ouch!

I didn't want to hear that. I liked it better when he was in the consoling mode—telling me everything would be OK.

I had the weekend to lick my wounds, but when Monday arrived, I still wasn't ready to face my boss. And honestly, I wasn't even sure I still had a job. I hadn't behaved very professionally.

I'd thought about it all weekend—what I would say to my boss, how I would explain my feelings, and how I would justify my actions. I couldn't lie and tell her I was OK with having someone else's name on the front of the books that I had written because I hated the idea. I felt hurt. I felt betrayed. I felt . . . convicted.

On the drive into the office, I heard that still small Voice speaking to me: *Would you be willing to write life-changing books for Me—even if no one ever knew that you wrote them?*

As tears streamed down my face, I realized that there was a part of me I had never given to God. All of my career aspirations and publishing dreams seemed too precious to hand over to Him.

I wrestled with myself during that drive into work, realizing it was one of those monumental moments in my life—a turning point. Was I going to write for me, or was I going to write for God?

As I parked my car, I prayed five simple words: "I work for You, God."

Immediately, I felt a weight lift from my heavy heart. I wiped my tears, and without hesitation I marched into my supervisor's office and asked to speak with her.

"Sure," she said, motioning for me to come in. "Have a seat."

"I'm sorry about the other day," I said. "Honestly, I don't care if you put 'written by Mickey Mouse' on the cover of these books. They are yours to do with what you want. I did write them on company time. And, it really shouldn't matter if I get credit for writing them. It's not about me. It's all about Him. I realize that now."

She smiled at me as I got up to leave, and then she hugged me. She'd never done that before.

"You know, you remind me a lot of myself when I was your age," she whispered. "I believe that God has big plans for you and your writing, but sometimes we have to go through the fire to get rid of all the impurities before we can go forward and walk fully in our callings" (see Malachi 3:2-3).

I knew what she meant. It wasn't that God couldn't use me with all of my imperfections. Of course He could. He's God. But she was letting me know that sometimes God allows "the fire" in our lives to reveal those areas we try and hide from Him, things that might keep us from walking fully in our callings.

In my case? It was pride.

Until the byline—my name—wasn't more important than glorifying His Name, I wouldn't be ready for bigger assignments. God couldn't trust me with more until I could trust Him more. And, you know what? I've discovered that God is the best boss of all because you can never out give God.

A few months after that incident, my boss dropped by my office and handed me a stack of papers.

"What's this?"

"Those are your stories," she said. "We've decided to go in a different direction, so you can have them back."

"Even though I wrote them on company time?"

"That's right," she said. "You're free to do whatever you want with them."

That next week, I sent off one of my stories to Ideals Children's Books. I chose to send *Conversations on the Ark*, the story of Noah's ark told from all of the animals' point-of-view. I'd read some of their Bible storybooks at Walmart, and it seemed like my children's book stories would fit nicely into their publishing program. Just a few weeks later, I got a call from Pat Pingry, a senior editor at Ideals at that time. She said she loved *Conversations on the Ark* and wanted to know if I had any more of those stories.

I totally did the dance of joy right there in my kitchen while still on the phone with Pat. (It's a good thing it wasn't a video call or I might've lost the contracts.)

Over the next few years, I sold *Conversations on the Ark*, *Memories of the Manger*, *The Sparrow's Easter Song*, and *Little Colt's Palm Sunday* to Ideals.

And, there's more! After my picture books came out, my company featured them in a two-page spread in the ministry Christmas catalog that went out to over five hundred thousand households. That one mailing sold thousands of copies of my books, making my publisher very happy and leading to many more book contracts.

Isn't that just like God? He always does more than we could ask or think—that's what the Word says in Ephesians 3:20. To date, I've published more than ninety books, and God continues to open publishing doors that amaze me. But I know I would never have seen any of my stories published if I hadn't trusted God with my career, if I hadn't remained moldable, if I hadn't allowed Him to deal with my pride. It wasn't an easy season, but it was a necessary one. I had to trust God with my children's stories, with my career, and ultimately with my life. I had to put my faith in Him and His plan, and that was scary. Sometimes, it still is.

How about you? Are there pieces of your life that you try to hide from God? Are you willing to let God take you in His hands and shape you?

THE MASTER'S TOUCH/THE PLATINUM PROCESS

My cousin Rudy Medlock is an amazing artist—especially when it comes to ceramics. In fact, he was my art professor when

I was a student at Asbury College. (I am pretty sure he gave me a C in Art History, which was the only C I received that semester. Not sure I've forgiven him yet for that, LOL.) But seriously, Rudy taught at Asbury for thirty-seven years, specializing in ceramics, sculpture, 3-D design, and stained glass. He has been working with ceramics and pottery since the 1960s. If you're ever blessed enough to stay at The Potter's Inn B and B (in Wilmore, Kentucky), owned and operated by Rudy and his lovely wife, Pat, you'll be able to see some of my cousin's gorgeous pottery. I received a piece as a wedding present, and I treasure it.

Because of Rudy's extensive knowledge, I recently asked him about the process of creating pottery so we could get a better understanding of this passage of scripture:

> *The word which came to Jeremiah from the* LORD *saying, "Arise and go down to the potter's house, and there I will announce My words to you." Then I went down to the potter's house, and there he was, making something on the wheel. But the vessel that he was making of clay was spoiled in the hand of the potter; so he remade it into another vessel, as it pleased the potter to make.*
>
> *Then the word of the* LORD *came to me saying, "Can I not, O house of Israel, deal with you as this potter does?" declares the* LORD. *"Behold, like the clay in the potter's hand, so are you in My hand."*
>
> (Jeremiah 18:1-6a NASB)

He explained that when you place the clay on the potter's wheel, you have to keep forcing the lump into the center, opening up the heart of it and lifting the clay as it spins in your hands.

"Occasionally," he said, "you'll find a foreign object or an air pocket in the piece, and you'll have to use a pin tool and remove the object or pop the air pocket before continuing in the process."

Then it's back to turning.

"As it's coming up, after you get rid of the imperfections, the piece might warp or become oval," he shared. "As the potter, you are steadily caressing it back to the center again to regain its original planned form."

This all takes place in the beginning steps of creating a ceramic piece. The potter doesn't rush it along because he knows if he does, the piece could suffer more imperfections or get off center.

It's just like us in the Master Potter's hands, isn't it? We can't rush through the process even though we'd like to get off the wheel as soon as possible because it's uncomfortable to be shaped and molded. But as we keep God at the center of our lives, the Master Potter will continue recentering us and removing any imperfections along the way.

The next part of the pottery process, according to Rudy, involves the hardening of the clay. Once you cut the piece off the wheel, it's time to dry, but if it dries too quickly, it can crack. In fact, Rudy said the drying process can take anywhere from a day to an entire week. Nothing can be rushed.

But if a piece cracks, a skilled potter can fix it by applying vinegar or some kind of moisture to the cracked area, working it back together with a varnishing tool until the crack becomes invisible. Then comes more drying, kiln time/bisque firing, glazing the piece, and back into the kiln for a final time. The potter waits for it to cool. Finally, he holds the finished product—a one-of-a-kind piece of beautiful pottery.

You see, we are never too off center or too broken for God. No chip, no crack, no break is too big for our God—the Master Potter—to restore. He simply puts us back onto the wheel and begins filling in, reshaping, and repairing our defects.

Of course, this analogy has its limitations. God doesn't cause the "fires" in our lives—such as cancer or divorce or bankruptcy—but in His mercy He *uses* them for our good, refining us in the process. I've walked through those times when I ended up back on the Potter's wheel, asking God to stop the pain and leave me alone with my imperfections, but He loves me too much to meet those requests. And, He loves you too much, as well. You know why? Because after He formed us, He put His initials on the bottom of our vessels. We are His! He created us!

That doesn't mean we will always understand what is happening or why He allows what He allows, but He is asking us to trust Him anyway. You see, faith is believing for the outcome you desire; platinum faith is still believing in God and following Him when the desired result doesn't happen.

PLATINUM PROPERTY

Platinum has many wonderful properties, which is why it's so useful as we discussed in chapter two, but one quality that makes it quite useful in jewelry making is its malleable nature, making it easy to shape and stretch.[1]

According to Dictionary.com, malleable is an adjective meaning "able to be hammered or pressed permanently out of shape without breaking or cracking." Synonyms include *pliable, workable, shapeable, moldable, cooperative, accommodating,* and *adaptable.* I want to be all of those things; don't you? I want God to mold me and shape me for His divine purposes.

PLATINUM PROMISE

The same way a potter can mold and shape clay into pots and mugs and decorative pieces, a jeweler can mold and shape platinum into ring settings or hammered pieces of platinum or stretch it into wire.

When we possess platinum faith, that means we give God permission to mold us and shape us however is needed. It means we allow Him to stretch us, even when it's uncomfortable. It means we trust Him throughout the whole process because we know He promises to work everything to good for those who love Him (Romans 8:28).

Just think. If we were able to view every negative situation in our lives as something that God could use to shape us into the vessels that He intended, maybe we could endure those painful seasons with much more grace. Then, we could begin to see our trials and struggles as opportunities for God to transform us.

Isaiah 64:8 says, "But now, O LORD, You are our Father, We are the clay, and You our potter; And all of us are the work of Your hand" (NASB).

I love that verse.

Praise God that we're in the Master Potter's hands.

Live Brilliant: The Importance of Stretching

BETHANY

The master potter takes a lot of time and effort to shape the clay the way he wants, and figuratively speaking, the clay has to be willing to be molded. Otherwise the clay remains in its original form, un-stretched and unpliable.

When I was an assistant cheerleading coach, the first thing we had the girls do before every practice or game was stretch. Their muscles needed to be warm so they wouldn't injure themselves. At the end of the practices, the head coach would always remind them to stretch at home. "You lose flexibility every day that you *don't* stretch."

Such an interesting thought.

Stretching our bodies can be uncomfortable, especially if you haven't tried to touch your toes in a while. Faith is the same way.

How many times have you felt God asking you to do something that wasn't comfortable? Awkward even?

In Scripture we see that God asks people to complete tasks that they often are not equipped for. Moses is called to ask Pharaoh to release the Israelites, yet Moses responded that he wasn't a man of words. David is called to be king, but as a lowly shepherd, he's unqualified. Paul was called to reach the Gentiles, but he was a persecutor of Christians.

Part of having a platinum faith means recognizing the voice of the Holy Spirit and being able to discern what God's will is. What if Moses refused to go to Pharaoh? What if David refused to be king? What if Paul refused to preach the gospel?

What if we refuse the call of God on our lives?

We can't be afraid to say yes when God stretches us in our faith because it's in the stretching that prepares us for the call.

If we want to be used by God and are willing to let our Master Potter mold us into the purpose He's called us for, then we have to be malleable.

We have to be pliable.

We have to stretch.

PLATINUM PROJECT

Take a moment to reflect on the seasons in your life when you experienced the most spiritual growth. Were they difficult seasons—times when you had to trust God just to survive? How did you grow or change? When was the last time you found yourself back on the Potter's wheel, being reshaped? Maybe you're experiencing that today. Let me encourage you to see this season through God's eyes—through the Master Potter's eyes—and celebrate the fact that you're on your way to platinum faith. Growing seasons are good seasons.

DISCUSSION QUESTIONS

1. Are there pieces of your life you try to hide from God, or are you willing to let him take you in His hands and shape you?

2. You lose flexibility with your faith every day that you don't stretch it. Have you ever felt God asking you to do something that wasn't comfortable? Did you allow Him to stretch you despite the discomfort, or did you stay in your comfort zone? If you stayed in your comfort zone, what was the main reason?

3. Take a moment to reflect on the seasons in your life when you experienced the most spiritual growth. How did you grow or change and what caused or encouraged it?

CHAPTER 9

You Can Resist Corrosion

BETHANY

Remember who you are. Don't compromise for anyone, for any reason. You are a child of the Almighty God. Live that truth.

Lysa Terkeurst

Journalism class was right after lunch. Juniors and seniors were allowed to go off campus and eat, which meant they were allowed to be anywhere they wanted to be as long as they came back at the appropriate time and weren't late for class.

Inevitably, this girl who lived in my neighborhood, which was only ten minutes from the school, would roll in a few minutes late, her blonde curly bob mussed in the back. A few minutes later her boyfriend would also arrive. It wasn't until I overheard a conversation the girl had with her friend that I realized what she was doing on her lunch break.

It wasn't going through the McDonald's drive-through, that's for certain.

And in my sheltered mind, I was surprised that she would admit to sleeping with her boyfriend. My family didn't talk about those types of behaviors, but here she was, openly sharing.

It made me wonder: did others do this on *their* lunch breaks?

I didn't have to wonder long. My boyfriend thought eating lunch at his house was a great idea, and the temptation to fool around is always present with teenage hormones raging. And despite my commitment to purity, I let things go to the point of "messing around without actually *messing* around."

And it became a cycle that I couldn't break.

I prayed to have the strength, but I felt beholden to my boyfriend, who was my ride *everywhere*, and I desperately longed to fit in and have friends. I felt alone in high school so I clung to my boyfriend. He was a built-in friend, and that brought a lot of comfort.

Now that I'm older, the Bible stories I grew up reading become clearer and I relate to the characters more.

Joseph, one of the more popular Bible characters, was often alone, too, and yet when he was faced with a woman who wanted to take their relationship to the next level, he resisted.

His faith was stronger than mine.

QUICK RESULTS OR SLOW FADE?

We're introduced to Joseph as a young man who is a major annoyance to his siblings:

> *Now Israel loved Joseph more than all his children, because he was the son of his old age. Also he made him a tunic of many colors. (Genesis 37:3 NKJV)*

The multicolored tunic represented a father's gift to his first-born son, as well as an indication of management-level status as opposed to those who labored.[1]

Jacob, Joseph's father, who stole his brother Esau's birthright as a younger man, is repeating a cycle. With his youngest son, Joseph, Jacob refuses to honor the tradition, the birthright of his oldest son, and any type of seniority.

But the brothers have had enough:

> *Now Joseph had a dream, and he told it to his brothers; and they hated him even more. (Genesis 37:5 NKJV)*

Despite the fact that his brothers hate him, Joseph can't help but brag about the dreams God gives him. Clearly, baby brother is basking in the favoritism not only from his earthly father Jacob but from his Heavenly Father, too.

But Joseph pushed the boundaries and told his brothers of a

second dream where they would bow down to him. And this time, Scripture says the brothers *envied him* (see Genesis 37:11).

Hatred.

Jealousy.

Two traits of corrosive behavior.

If I were Joseph, I'm not so sure I could have handled the situation and come out the other side with forgiveness. He was sold as a slave to merchants who sold him to Potiphar, an officer in Pharaoh's household. We don't know if Joseph ever tried to escape, but the Bible says that it was due to Joseph's character that he rose in favor and was promoted to the highest position with Potiphar.

In fact, Scripture says that the Lord was with Joseph, which indicates that despite his circumstances, Joseph held on to God and God blessed him and helped him rise in favor.

But this is the part of the story where things get a bit *Desperate Housewives*.

When Joseph worked in Potiphar's house is where we see a platinum faith in the making.

PLATINUM PROPERTY

Platinum is such an interesting metal. One of the reasons it's so valuable is because it is extremely resistant to corrosion, the process in which a chemical is gradually destroyed by another chemical or by its environment.

It doesn't oxidize in air at any temperature, unlike an avocado, which turns brown thirty seconds after cutting it open. However, platinum is not completely corrosion-proof. There are some chemicals that will cause it to corrode, including halogens and sulfur.[2] Even though these elements are corrosive, they come disguised as beneficial.

Halogens are highly toxic and reactive, although in small doses they keep our pearly whites safe from cavities. And anytime

I hear the word *sulfur* I think immediately of an old egg smell, but sulfur is necessary for human life to exist because our bodies need it for dietary reasons.

Two corrosive elements that are beneficial in small doses. Comparatively, how many times do we maintain friendships with toxic people because even though they hurt us, we can see the good in them?

The company we keep can cause our personalities, our emotions, the essence of *who we are* to go downhill. The Bible says to be careful of who we hang around. Proverbs 12:26 says, "The righteous choose their friends carefully, but the way of the wicked leads them astray." We become like the people we hang around the most. We take on their mannerisms, expressions, and habits.

The bottom line is that we become like the company we keep, so we need to be careful. If we're holding onto relationships that aren't edifying, it can actually hurt our chances at future relationships. The Bible says, "Walk with the wise and become wise, for a companion of fools suffers harm" (Proverbs 13:20 NIV).

During a high school youth camp main session, some performers demonstrated how negative behavior can have a stronger effect on us than positive behavior. One person representing "the good influence" stood on a chair. The person representing "the bad influence" stood next to him. The kid on the chair was instructed to pull the other kid onto the chair with him. He tried—he really did, especially since fifteen hundred pairs of eyes were watching to see if he could actually do it.

Needless to say, he couldn't pull the kid onto the chair. Scientifically, the leverage wasn't there (or whatever the actual scientific principle that would apply).

Then the kid on the stage was instructed to pull the kid standing on the chair *off* the chair.

Took him two seconds.

The point was made. It's harder to bring someone up to a

positive level than it is to bring someone down to a negative one.

I've found this true in my own life. Attempting to be the positive role model sets you up to be the goody-two-shoes, the prude, the stick-in-the-mud, or as my husband lovingly teases me, the "fun sponge."

However, the Bible says that wise people become wise by walking with those who are wise (Proverbs 13:20). We might lose out on the best friendships we'd ever known if we're hanging out with foolish people.

This is not to say that we shouldn't love or be friends with people who aren't wise or godly. By all means, we see by Jesus's example that He chose to build relationships with people whom society considered to be the outcasts. But here's the kicker: those people weren't Jesus's best friends.

Jesus had thousands of disciples, but His closest circle of friends were the twelve apostles (although Judas may shift that number from twelve to eleven—*eek*). The twelve apostles can be broken down into a smaller group: Peter, James, and John. And then we have John: the one whom Jesus loved, as he refers to himself all throughout his Gospel.

Having a platinum faith means that we are careful to surround ourselves with people who love us, speak life over us, and edify us so that we can avoid any type of corrosive influence in our hearts.

But what about the people in our lives we can't get away from?

PLATINUM PROMISE

Let's jump back to shepherd boy Joseph's story. He was loved by his father, hated by his brothers, sold to merchants, and then sold to Potiphar, the second highest officer in the land of Egypt.

The blessing of God was upon Joseph, and he found favor and trust in Potiphar's house.

And after a time, Potiphar's wife takes notice of handsome Joseph and unabashedly comes on to him. It probably wasn't the first time she'd had her way with a servant in the household, but it was probably the first time the servant turned her down.

And despite Joseph's refusal, she persisted. And with every refusal, I can only imagine that her desire to sleep with Joseph was replaced with a desire to win this game of cat and mouse, to prove that she was desirable, to fill a void within her own life, and definitely to fill a void in her soul.

Scripture says that Joseph not only refused to sleep with her but also ignored her and stayed away from her.

And that ate at her spirit.

When Justin and I were dating, we had a couple of rocky times in our relationship when we were temporarily broken up. During the second of these breakups, another guy started paying attention to me. As I was feeling neglected by my boyfriend, I welcomed his attention.

Until that guy was no longer interested.

And I found myself doing the one thing I swore I would never ever, ever do.

I pursued him.

One morning I was feeling particularly lonely and unlovable, still missing Justin but not willing to make amends or admit that I loved him. The frustration that this other guy had *not* chased me the way I'd expected him to bothered me, and in an effort to prove to myself that I was desirable, I marched across the college campus, knocked on his door, waited forever for him to answer, only to be told he didn't want to hang out.

Desperation for attention turned into humiliation, and I cursed myself for being the stupid girl doing the equivalent of waiting at home all night by the phone for a call that didn't come, only to call the boy herself and find out he never intended to call.

The bottom fell out of my heart, and I hated myself in that moment.

I wonder if Potiphar's wife felt the same way. Undesired by the man she desired. Humiliated and rejected in her own home.

The Bible says to resist even the appearance of evil, and Joseph fell victim to an unfortunate circumstance. One day, Joseph is minding his master's business, enters the house, and Potiphar's wife tries again, close enough to him that she grabs his clothes. With no witness, no men in the house, Joseph flees, and his clothes—or part of his clothes—are left in her hands.

He resisted temptation.

He did the right thing, but Potiphar's wife accused him of treachery, and he was thrown into prison.

He lost everything.

Joseph's story proves that having a platinum faith doesn't mean that life always works out great. In fact, many times doing the right thing, sticking to your guns, following the Lord's lead, can mean that you end up in what you consider to be *worse* circumstances than you intended. Potiphar's wife was toxic, and Joseph's life took a negative spiral. But God was still with Joseph. Despite his terrible situation, Joseph resisted corrosion.

If we continue into Joseph's story, we see how God used Joseph's imprisonment to get him to Pharaoh. It was because of this terrible situation that Joseph became second in command to the prison keeper, then to Pharaoh himself.

The lesson here is simple, though painful. Doing the right thing is always the right thing no matter what the consequences *because God can bless obedience.*

In fact, a mantra I used to say to myself when I was faced with temptation was just that: God can bless my obedience, but He can't bless my disobedience. In other words, I know that God can work through my disobedience, but it isn't pleasing to Him.

We can set up safeguards to help prevent us from coming too close to dangerous situations. Don't play with matches and your chances of burning down the house decrease dramatically. Always wearing a seatbelt can reduce the risk of injury in a car crash. The seatbelt doesn't stop the crash from happening but lessens the likelihood of extreme damage to your body.

James 3:1-12 is dedicated to teaching us to tame our tongues. With our tongues we both bless and curse, so we must learn to control it.

A friend of mine got really mad at me over a social media comment a few years ago. *Ever been there?* I hadn't meant any harm and apologized. But my friend was dealing with issues behind the scenes, and my comment was the spark that ignited the kindling of hurt that was brewing under the surface.

She overreacted, lashed out, and questioned my integrity and my faith. It wasn't pretty.

As a result, our relationship was never the same, and it has not been an easy road to travel.

Being resistant to corrosion means keeping anything that could erode at your spirit far away—not even giving it a chance to do harm.

James 3:14-16 describes what corrosive behavior looks like and where we find its source:

> But if you have bitter jealousy and selfish ambition in your hearts, do not boast and be false to the truth. This is not the wisdom that comes down from above, but is earthly, unspiritual, demonic. For where jealousy and selfish ambition exist, there will be disorder and every vile practice. (ESV)

If we are striving toward platinum faith, we have to recognize the characteristics that can destroy us, like jealousy, pride, and greed. Thankfully, the Bible tells us how to resist this corrosion. James 3:17-18 continues:

> But the wisdom from above is first pure, then peaceable, gentle, open to reason, full of mercy and good fruits, impartial and sincere. And a harvest of righteousness is sown in peace by those who make peace. (ESV)

Peace.

We must find peace, create peace, and sow peace, no matter how ugly someone is to us.

Live Brilliant:
No More Offense!

MICHELLE

When I ponder platinum faith—a faith that is resistant to corrosion—I can't help thinking about one particular woman who still inspires me today.

I honestly don't remember what her specific talk was about that afternoon, but I do remember what she said in response to some accusations a famous evangelist had directed toward her—an evangelist who didn't approve of female ministers. Knowing we'd probably all read of his verbal attacks on her, she obviously felt she should address the "elephant in the room" before diving into her talk. I was ready for her to go off on a righteous rant, and we all would've backed her and probably "amen-ed" her a few times, but that's not what she did. Instead, she said this:

"I'm not mad at him for saying what he said against me; I'm mad that my heart reacted to what he said. I'm mad that I felt offense toward him because I thought I'd grown enough in my faith to no longer let those kinds of things affect me."

In essence, she was saying, "I'm mad that I let his hurtful words corrode my heart."

That totally blew me away. She had every right to be angry at this man for saying such ridiculous remarks about her in the media, and yet, that's not what upset her. She was upset his remarks had affected her at all.

Now, that's platinum faith.

I also desire to get to the place where I don't let insignificant things corrode my heart. Offense is such a tough one. It's so easy to get our feelings hurt and allow offense to take root in our hearts, isn't it? Here's the problem. Offense doesn't set up camp all by itself. It usually brings along bitterness and anger, too.

Proverbs 19:11 says, "Good sense makes one slow to anger, and it is his glory to overlook an offense" (ESV).

It's to his glory to overlook an offense. That's reason enough right there to stop being offended, isn't it? Yet I realize, it's easier said than done. None of us wants to become offended, but it happens sometimes. However, if we wish to do big things for God and make an impact for the kingdom, you can bet the enemy will set "offense traps" as we walk this journey of faith. You see, the devil doesn't want us accomplishing things for God and knows if he can keep us offended, we'll never be very effective. So, let's stay prayed up and ready! Let's ask God to fill us up with so much love there isn't room for any offense.

PLATINUM PROJECT

Taking a long hard look at the company we keep isn't easy. It's hard to list the faults and weaknesses of others without seeing some of those same negative qualities in ourselves. But there is a distinction between having friends who build you up and having frenemies who tear you down.

Pray for discernment and wisdom. We must first examine our own hearts and ask God to show us where we need forgiveness so we can be forgiven before forgiving others. Ask God to show you where corrosion threatens to destroy your faith and then be willing to make changes when He reveals those areas.

May we all ask God for His strength so that we can be strong enough to resist corrosion and continue to live out a platinum faith.

DISCUSSION QUESTIONS

1. Joseph's story in Scripture proves that having platinum faith doesn't mean life will always work out great. Despite his terrible situation, God was still with Joseph, who continued to resist corrosion. In the end, God blessed his obedience. Do you find it easy or hard to avoid corrosive influences? How do you handle corrosive people you can't avoid?

2. Do you tend to get offended or are you able to let offenses go without responding to them?

3. Before we forgive others, we must first examine our own hearts and ask God to show us where we need forgiveness so we can be forgiven. Are you still holding on to hidden sin or un-forgiveness? Ask God to show you where corrosion threatens to destroy your faith and then be willing to make changes when He reveals those areas.

CHAPTER 10

You Can Replace Your Heavy Heart with God's Heavy Presence

MICHELLE

For you and me, just knowing His presence is all around us can help lift us from the darkest night, embrace us in the loneliest hour, give us strength when we are tempted, and enable us to live confident and secure in His promises.

Diane H. Moody

When my oldest daughter, Abby, came home from college her sophomore year and told me she had fallen in love with a young man named Micah who felt called to ministry, I was thrilled. I'd never seen her face light up the way it did when she spoke about Micah. She was radiant. So happy. So in love. And, the thought of Abby and Micah ministering together thrilled this mama's soul—for a moment.

She continued, "Mom, he thinks he will eventually go abroad and minister. He feels called to missions."

Wait, what?

"And, if we're going to plan a future together," she said, "then I have to be OK with all of that. If he's called, I'm called. I need you to be OK with all that, too."

I nodded, breathed deeply, and hugged her, searching for words.

"Of course," I said. "If God's in it, I'm for it!"

Those were the words she needed to hear, so I said them, but I didn't feel them.

I retreated to my bedroom closet and had a good cry, begging God, "Please don't take my daughter overseas for long periods of time."

The thought of having future grandchildren in some far-off land, never getting to see them, pierced my heart in a way I'd never felt before. I knew it was selfish of me to feel this way. After all, many families go through separation when their loved ones are called to serve on the mission field, in the military, in the peace corps, or in another noble way. Yet, I couldn't pretend that my heart wasn't heavy. I could hardly breathe from the overwhelming heaviness.

It was fear. Major fear.

Eventually, I began to feel His peace replace that heaviness as I stayed in His presence. The verse, "Cast your cares on the LORD," kept rising up in my spirit (Psalm 55:22). I prayed, "Lord, I give You my fears. I ask that You calm my heart concerning Abby's and Micah's future and guide them, Lord, into the future You have for them. Don't let me stand in the way, Father."

We had dedicated Abby to God when she was a baby, in front of our entire church, yet at times like this, I wanted to take her back and protect her. I wanted to keep her close. Still, I knew God loved her even more than I did, and I could trust Him. He would never leave her or forsake her, either.

Today, Abby and Micah are serving in ministry in Lexington, Kentucky. Micah is the Worship Arts minister, and he and Abby lead several small groups. The other night, they had over thirty college-aged kids at their home for Bible study. I love that so much.

I don't know if they'll ever go overseas to serve, but if they do, I will cast that burden on the Lord. I have learned that carrying it myself is way too hard and heavy and miserable. His yoke is easy, and His burden is light.

How about you? What are you carrying today? What part of your heart have you hidden from God, hoping He won't notice? What is weighing you down?

It's time to cast your cares. It's time to replace your heavy heart with God's heavy presence.

PLATINUM PROPERTY

As metals go, platinum is heavy. In fact, it is close to 60 percent heavier than gold, which is also a weighty metal, and platinum is 30 percent heavier than silver. Though you probably don't shop with a jeweler's scale or any type of lab equipment to measure a piece of jewelry's weight—to see if it's platinum or not—you can tell simply by holding it in your hand. It feels heavier. The rule of thumb is, if it feels too heavy to be silver, it's probably platinum.[1]

Simply put, platinum is heavy. It's weighty. When you put on a piece of platinum jewelry, you know you're wearing it. Its presence is tangible the entire time you're wearing it, not in an annoying way, but in an "I feel it there" way. Much like the tangible presence of God.

It's weighty. You're aware it's there.

Throughout the Bible, we read about people being so over-whelmed by His presence, they aren't able to move under the weight of it. Take Daniel, for example. God gives him a vision of the ram and the goat, and as he tries to understand what he has just seen, he encounters God's tangible presence and falls to the ground, on his face, in what he could only describe as a deep sleep:

> While I, Daniel, was watching the vision and trying to understand it, there before me stood one who looked like a man. And I heard a man's voice from the Ulai calling, "Gabriel, tell this man the meaning of the vision."
>
> As he came near the place where I was standing, I was terrified and fell prostrate. "Son of man," he said to me, "understand that the vision concerns the time of the end." While he was speaking to me, I was in a deep sleep, with my face to the ground. (Daniel 8:15-18)

Daniel experiences the same thing in chapter 10:

> On the twenty-fourth day of the first month, as I was standing on the bank of the great river, the Tigris, I looked up and there before me was a man dressed in linen, with a belt of fine gold from Uphaz around his waist. His body was like topaz, his face like lightning, his eyes like flaming

torches, his arms and legs like the gleam of burnished bronze, and his voice like the sound of a multitude.

I, Daniel, was the only one who saw the vision; those who were with me did not see it, but such terror overwhelmed them that they fled and hid themselves. So I was left alone, gazing at this great vision; I had no strength left, my face turned deathly pale and I was helpless. Then I heard him speaking, and as I listened to him, I fell into a deep sleep, my face to the ground. (Daniel 10:4-9)

When Solomon dedicated the temple, the priests couldn't even enter because the glory of God filled it. His presence was so dense and heavy that they could not set foot inside the temple:

When Solomon finished praying, fire came down from heaven and consumed the burnt offering and the sacrifices, and the glory of the LORD filled the temple. The priests could not enter the temple of the LORD because the glory of the LORD filled it. When all the Israelites saw the fire coming down and the glory of the LORD above the temple, they knelt on the pavement with their faces to the ground, and they worshipped and gave thanks to the LORD, saying, "He is good; his love endures forever." (2 Chronicles 7:1-3)

I believe the Israelites knelt on the pavement, their faces to the ground, because God's glory was so present and so heavy, they weren't able to stand.

In Ezekiel, chapter one, we read about his inaugural vision that ends with him facedown in the presence of Almighty God:

I saw that from what appeared to be his waist up he looked like glowing metal, as if full of fire, and that from there down he looked like fire; and brilliant light surrounded him. Like the appearance of a rainbow in the clouds on a rainy day, so was the radiance around him. This was the appearance of the likeness of the glory of the LORD. When I saw it, I fell facedown, and I heard the voice of one speaking. (Ezekiel 1:27-28)

Ezekiel once again comes in contact with God's glory in chapter three, and again he drops to the ground:

> The hand of the LORD was on me there, and he said to me, "Get up and go out to the plain, and there I will speak to you." So I got up and went out to the plain. And the glory of the LORD was standing there, like the glory I had seen by the Kebar River, and I fell facedown. (Ezekiel 3:22-23)

Ezekiel falls to the ground two more times in response to God's glory in chapters 43 and 44!

I guess we shouldn't be surprised that the Hebrew word for "glory" is *kavod*, which means the "weight or heaviness" of God. Nor should we be surprised that when it comes upon you, it causes you to collapse under its weight.[2]

Live Brilliant:
Walk by Faith, Not by Sight

BETHANY

Kavod is an amazing word. Along with "heaviness," it can also be translated as "respect," "dignity," or "honor." Rabbi Shalom Wolbe is quoted as saying, "Kavod is external behavior mandated by and appropriate to a reality of inner holiness. Behold, you have within you a *Tzelem Elokim Kadosh* (holy divine image)—this requires you to treat yourself with a certain level of self-respect."[3]

Interestingly, *kavod* is also translated "glory." The glory of God is depicted several times in the Old Testament, but one of my favorites is when God led the Israelites out of Egypt.

"By day the LORD went ahead of them in a pillar of cloud to guide them on their way and by night in a pillar of fire to give them light, so that they could travel by day or night. Neither the pillar of cloud by day nor the pillar of fire by night left its place in front of the people" (Exodus 13:21-22 NIV).

These pillars of fire and clouds were the manifestation of God in physical form. Because even though we know God is with us, we sometimes still need to *see*.

This is in contrast with the exhortation from Paul in 2 Corinthians 5:7, "For we live by faith, not by sight" (NIV).

Not we *should* live by faith and not sight, but that we *already do.*

I would love to be able to see God's glory, whether it be a pillar of clouds, pillar of fire, or in a bush that burns but does not burn up. But I have something that the Israelites did not have: the inner dwelling of the Holy Spirit. And one day we'll be with God in heaven and be able to see Jesus face-to-face.

And if we look closely enough at God's creation, we can see His fingerprints clearly pressed upon the fabric of the universe.

So we honor God by living lives worthy of our calling, by honoring others in our lives: our parents, our spouses, our friends, other Christians, and our children: "Let love be genuine. Abhor what is evil; hold fast to what is good. Love one another with brotherly affection. Outdo one another in showing honor. Do not be slothful in zeal, be fervent in spirit, serve the Lord. Rejoice in hope, be patient in tribulation, be constant in prayer. Contribute to the needs of the saints and seek to show hospitality" (Romans 12:9-13 ESV).

And we honor God by respecting ourselves. We are created in God's image, His crown of creation. First Corinthians 6:20: "For you were bought with a price. So glorify God in your body" (ESV).

Let's cast off the negative self-talk, the self-abuse, and the self-loathing. All three of those things begin with the same prefix: *self-*. Let's focus on the calling God's placed in life, and by doing so, show Him the full honor that He deserves.

THE HEAVY PRESENCE OF GOD

I've actually experienced *kavod*, succumbing to the heavy presence of Almighty God, one time twenty-five years ago, and it changed my life forever.

When I was only eleven weeks pregnant with our second baby, I was leaving the YMCA in Bloomington, Indiana, after teaching a low-impact aerobics class, when pain shot through my abdomen. The dull cramping I'd felt a little earlier was becoming more intense. I knew something was wrong.

Turns out, I wasn't only cramping; I was bleeding.

I drove straight to my OB-GYN and through tears explained what was going on. After an exam and what seemed like hours, the doctor said very matter-of-factly that I was in the process of miscarrying my baby.

"Go home and rest with your feet up, and if you pass it before Monday, go to the ER."

I stared at him blankly, completely in shock.

"That's it? There's nothing you can do?"

"I'm afraid not," he said, patting me on the back. "These things happen."

The entire drive home, the doctor's words kept replaying in my head. He'd gone on to tell me that miscarriages in the first trimester were very common, that statistics show as many as one in four women miscarry early on. Many don't even know they've suffered a miscarriage because it happens so early, he'd explained. They think they're just having a heavy period.

These things happen.

I kept hearing those words, but I couldn't wrap my heart around them, because these things didn't happen to me. I wasn't just a statistic. My baby wasn't just a "thing" to pass.

Lying on our couch with my feet up, per doctor's orders, I couldn't help but think, *This can't be it. This can't be the end of the story.*

"Sis!" my older sister, Martie, called, making her way through the house. "Mom just told me."

Martie listened to me relay the horrible diagnosis, and then she said, "Get up and get ready. You're coming to church with us tonight."

"I can't go anywhere," I answered, kind of aggravated she'd even ask. "Did you not just hear what the doctor said I had to do?"

"Yes, I heard," she continued. "But I know you and Jeff are supposed to go with us to hear this evangelist tonight."

Knowing my sister would never take no for an answer, I got up and got ready. So, my parents, my sister and her husband, and Jeff and I went to a revival service in downtown Bedford to hear an evangelist I knew nothing about in a place I'd never been before. And, we were running late to add even more stress to an already-stressful situation. As we slipped into the back row, the evangelist looked our way and said, "I've been waiting for you."

Not going to lie—I was a little embarrassed, figuring he'd called us out for coming in late. I tried to listen as he preached, but I kept thinking about my baby. I looked down at my belly that had no sign of a baby bump yet and wondered if this miscarriage was my fault for teaching low-impact aerobics that day. Just then, the evangelist stopped his message, got very quiet, and said, "Someone here has been told you are going to miscarry your baby today, and I'm here to tell you that's a lie from the pit of hell. Come up here. I want to pray for you."

I froze—unable to move at all—wondering if he was talking about me or if possibly another woman could have received my same dismal diagnosis.

Just then, a woman across the room stood up, and he said to her, "Ma'am, you're not the one God showed me, but I will pray for you."

"I think he's talking about you," Jeff whispered in my ear.

I knew he was, but I still couldn't move.

Could this be real? Could this be for me? Could this be God?

Before I could think another thought, the evangelist walked all the way to the back of the room, grabbed my hand, and led me down front. Hot tears filled my eyes and my throat. I felt like I might pass out.

That evangelist pointed right at my belly and said, "I declare today that your little girl will live and not die and declare the works of the Lord! And you will not have any more trouble with this pregnancy!"

Little girl? I'm having another girl?

Immediately, I felt an intense warmth flow through my body. It was so overwhelming, so unlike anything I'd ever felt before—so heavy—I fell to the ground. Well, actually I fell forward, right on top of the evangelist, I later learned. But I don't remember any of that. All I remember is lying there with what felt like a heavy, warm blanket covering me. I couldn't move, but I didn't want to. In fact, I could've stayed there forever because I knew God was all over me in a way I'd only read about, never before experienced.

I'd heard ministers refer to God's anointing as being "heavy," but at that moment, I physically knew what they meant.

Much of the next half hour is a blur for me, but I remember lying there, knowing that God had restored my pregnancy, knowing that I was having a baby girl, and knowing that she would live and not die and declare the works of the Lord.

On Monday, my doctor's appointment confirmed what I already knew—there was a strong heartbeat, and it belonged to my baby girl.

Allyson Michelle Adams was born on August 15, 1994, and she truly is mighty for God.

PLATINUM PROMISE

I walked into that church service with a very heavy heart, knowing I'd probably never get to hold my baby.

But God.

While there, I encountered the heavy presence of Almighty God—Jehovah Rapha, God, My Healer—and I left that service feeling restored, free, happy . . . light. You see, I'd encountered God in a way I'd never experienced before, and I traded my heavy heart for His heavy anointing.

Of course, we don't have to feel God's presence for Him to work in our lives. But, sometimes, we do "feel" His presence. Here's the key—we have to know that He is with us, whether we "feel" Him or not. We go by faith, not feeling.

We are assured of that truth. In fact, the Word says He is *in* us! "And Christ lives within you, so even though your body will die because of sin, the Spirit gives you life because you have been made right with God" (Romans 8:10 NLT).

And, Galatians 2:20 tells us, "My old self has been crucified with Christ. It is no longer I who live, but Christ lives in me" (NLT).

Not only does He live in us, but He promises to never leave us! Genesis 28:15 says, "What's more, I am with you, and I will protect you wherever you go. One day I will bring you back to this land. I will not leave you until I have finished giving you everything I have promised you" (NLT).

And, Hebrews 13:5 says, "Never will I leave you; never will I forsake you."

God is always with us.

Talk about a platinum promise!

Here's more good news: though His anointing is heavy, His burden is light. Jesus encourages us to give Him our heavy burdens. He can take it. We were never meant to carry them alone.

"Then Jesus said, 'Come to me, all of you who are weary and carry heavy burdens, and I will give you rest. Take my yoke upon you. Let me teach you, because I am humble and gentle at heart, and you will find rest for your souls. For my yoke is easy to bear, and the burden I give you is light'" (Matthew 11:28-30 NLT).

No matter what you're going through today. No matter what

heavy news you might've just received. No matter how tired you are from fighting through life. God's got you. He says to cast all of your cares and anxieties on Him (1 Peter 5:7)!

So, let's do that right now.

PLATINUM PROJECT

Take a moment and grab your prayer journal or simply find a piece of paper and write down all of the burdens you've been carrying around like a pack mule. Now, lift that list up to God in faith, and pray:

"Father God, I praise You for Who You are and for all You've done and are going to do. I love You so much. Lord, I come to You today, casting all my cares upon You, just as Your Word instructs. Every single thing on my list, Father, I give to You. I'm weary and sometimes I'm scared, so I'm asking that You remove the burdens and infuse me with Your strength and love. Thank You for replacing my heavy heart with Your heavy presence. Help me to walk in platinum faith, aware of Your presence, as I carry out the plans You have for my life. Thank You, Lord, for promising to never leave me. Thank You for living in me and guiding me into Your perfect will. I love You. I trust You. And, I commit myself to You in a new and mighty way. In the Name of Your Precious Son, Amen."

DISCUSSION QUESTIONS

1. What burdens are you carrying, and what part of your heart have you hidden from God?

2. Throughout Scripture, God's presence shows up as weighty, heavy, and overwhelming (in a good way). Has there been a time when you traded a heavy heart for a heavy anointing? If so, how did your life change?

3. We honor God by respecting ourselves and focusing on the calling He has placed on our lives. Are you still holding on to "self" in some way? Take time to reflect and ask God what you need to relinquish to Him.

CHAPTER 11

You Are Special

BETHANY

If something isn't special, then it's ordinary.

Nora Roberts

Because I'm a people-pleaser, I often let people walk all over me. I lose my voice and give up control just to make them happy. I always feel gross about it afterwards.

A few years ago, my husband, Justin, and I were hosting a multiday get-together at our house. To make sure our guests were comfortable, I asked for meal preferences and allergies and spent extra money on special snacks to ensure a wonderful and hospitable experience. Justin told me I was going overboard, but I wanted to impress these people, so I threw myself into the planning.

I should have listened.

All my preparation started to unravel the morning after our guests arrived. They didn't like the brand of waffles I'd bought, so before breakfast they went to the grocery store. And it just went downhill from there. Every meal was criticized, each activity scrutinized, and I felt smaller and smaller under their microscopic judgment. Five hundred little frustrating incidents happened that weekend, and I felt like a ticking time bomb, anxious and stressed.

Instead of confronting the bad behavior, I allowed myself to be mistreated. In my own home. And even to this day, I'm still ashamed that I let it go on.

We devalue our worth when we don't speak up for ourselves.

Why do we act like that? Is it because of some need to feel important to someone, even if that person treats us with disrespect?

Because that's not how God sees us. We are His daughters and

He loves us so much that He sent His Son to die for us. In a sense we're God's "commodity," and our value is priceless.

PLATINUM PROPERTY

Platinum is a commodity, which can mean a couple of things. First, a commodity can be bought or sold, and second, it can mean something that is precious or valuable.[1] As we've mentioned in other chapters, platinum is a highly sought-after metal. It's ironic when you think about it. Platinum is both special and exploited.

And so often, people are treated the same way. Human trafficking is a hundreds-of-billions-of-dollars-a-year "industry" that dehumanizes the victims and is one of the most despicable, vile, and loathsome evils in this world.

When we feel broken, we sometimes trade parts of ourselves to other people—emotionally *and* physically. During my time as a youth minister's wife and high school cheerleading coach I witnessed firsthand some of the girls struggling with their desire to keep their boyfriend *and* their virtue, always wondering where the line was before they crossed into questionable territory. And I watched as girl after girl gave too much of her heart and body to a boy who took those pieces and crushed them.

When we explore the Scriptures, we see that feeling not special isn't a twenty-first-century problem.

UNWANTED

Leah, the unwanted wife of Jacob, along with her father, Laban, may be the original "catfishers."

If you've never seen the popular reality TV show *Catfish*, hosts Nev and Max travel around the country to help people meet in person their online boyfriend or girlfriend. Many times the relationship has developed strictly through e-mails or texts with zero video chats, FaceTime, or even talking on the phone, which seems a bit *fishy* if you're in love with someone.

After watching a few episodes of the show, you notice that a disturbing pattern emerges.

A pattern that breaks your heart.

Many times, the *catfish*, aka the person on the other side of the screen, is so damaged, so hurt, so insecure, that the only way that person feels confident is to hide behind a mask by using someone else's pictures to create a new virtual life. Way too often that person is living in the wake of abuse or bullying and is so self-focused and self-centered, this damaged individual doesn't take the time to really think about the consequences of their actions. They're not valuing the other person's feelings.

Catfish reminds me of the film *You've Got Mail*, which I said was the original "catfish movie" until my mom reminded me that *You've Got Mail* is actually a remake of the 1940s *Shop Around the Corner*. In *You've Got Mail*, Meg Ryan and Tom Hanks play two competing shop owners.

They meet in a chat room and begin an online relationship. Halfway through the movie, Hanks figures out that Ryan is the girl behind the computer and, without her knowing, continues to talk to her and progress their relationship.

The movie is a popular romantic comedy that ends with Ryan and Hanks happily ever after, but when the scenario is played out in real life, the ending isn't always so pretty.

Jacob, the twin brother of Esau, has left his hometown and gone to meet with his uncle Laban. When Jacob arrives, he sees his cousin Rachel and immediately begins marriage negotiations with Laban:

> Then Laban said to Jacob, "Because you are my kinsman,
> should you therefore serve me for nothing? Tell me, what
> shall your wages be?" Now Laban had two daughters. The
> name of the older was Leah, and the name of the younger
> was Rachel. Leah's eyes were weak, but Rachel was beau-
> tiful in form and appearance. Jacob loved Rachel. And
> he said, "I will serve you seven years for your younger

daughter Rachel." Laban said, "It is better that I give her
to you than that I should give her to any other man; stay
with me." So Jacob served seven years for Rachel, and
they seemed to him but a few days because of the love he
had for her. (Genesis 29:15-20 ESV)

According to the NIV Application Commentary, marriage
contracts were typical in those days: "In texts from Nuzi the
typical bride price was thirty to forty shekels. Since a shepherd's
annual wage was ten shekels a year, Jacob is in effect paying a
premium by working seven years, but he is in no position to
negotiate."[2]

The Bible says that Jacob worked those seven years, but
because of his love for Rachel, they felt like only a few days. His
time was up, he'd paid his price, and now he wanted to marry the
love of his life:

So Laban gathered together all the people of the place and
made a feast. But in the evening he took his daughter Leah
and brought her to Jacob, and he went in to her.
(Genesis 29:22-23 ESV)

It was customary for the bride to be covered, or veiled,
during these ceremonies. Scripture says that "in the evening"
Laban took Leah to Jacob. Can we assume, then, that Rachel was
veiled during the wedding feast? That she thought it was to be
her wedding night? When Laban took Leah to Jacob, did Rachel
protest? Why didn't she run screaming his name so he wouldn't
make this grave mistake?

We simply don't know. We only know that in the morning,
Jacob realized he'd been tricked:

And in the morning, behold, it was Leah! And Jacob said
to Laban, "What is this you have done to me? Did I not
serve with you for Rachel? Why then have you deceived
me?" Laban said, "It is not so done in our country, to give
the younger before the firstborn." (Genesis 29:25-26 ESV)

Let's consider.

Seven years is a long time. It's safe to say that Jacob got to know Rachel and her sister Leah during his time working for Laban. Neither woman would have been a stranger to him. And yet during these seven years, Leah is never married.

We don't know much about Leah before she married Jacob, but we do know that she slept with the man who loved her sister. If she thought this treachery would make her happy or give her the comfort of provision and protection she needed from a husband, she was sorely mistaken.

Jacob finished his honeymoon week with Leah and immediately married Rachel, then worked another seven years for Laban. I don't think this set of seven years flew by as fast as the first did for Jacob:

> When the LORD saw that Leah was hated, he opened her womb, but Rachel was barren. (Genesis 29:31 ESV)

Unwanted Leah became unloved Leah, a commodity in her father's games.

PLATINUM PROMISE: KNOW YOUR WORTH

We weren't meant to be treated disrespectfully.

We weren't created to be pawns in people's games.

We are daughters of the true King.

Bethany. Daughter of Elohim.

Michelle. Daughter of God Almighty.

You. Daughter of the One true God.

Jesus's sacrifice, the blood He shed, the price He paid meant something. It *means* something.

When we tear ourselves down and beat ourselves up, we're destroying something valuable. Something special.

First Corinthians 6:20 says we were bought at a price and are to honor our bodies (ESV). Maybe you've felt unloved and unwanted like Leah. Maybe you've felt like no one cared and that you didn't matter.

Maybe someone hurt you and the pain lingers deep in the dark corners of your heart and soul.

Never mistake abuse for love:

> *There is no fear in love, but perfect love casts out fear. For fear has to do with punishment, and whoever fears has not been perfected in love. (1 John 4:18 ESV)*

Abandonment and abuse are never ever God's will. We can't know why some terrible and heinous acts are *allowed* to happen to us, and we may never know this side of heaven. The Bible tells us that you and I are precious, worthy, and wanted:

> *See what kind of love the Father has given to us, that we should be called children of God; and so we are.*
> *(1 John 3:1a ESV)*

> *I have been crucified with Christ. It is no longer I who live, but Christ who lives in me. And the life I now live in the flesh I live by faith in the Son of God, who loved me and gave himself for me. (Galatians 2:20 ESV)*

And one of my favorites:

> *But God shows his love for us in that while we were still sinners, Christ died for us. (Romans 5:8 ESV)*

We are children of God.
Not pawns to be played with.
Not commodities to be exploited.
Special.
Forgiven.
Loved.

Live Brilliant:
Know Your Worth,
Respect Others' Worth

MICHELLE

"The tongue has the power of life and death, and those who love it will eat its fruit." (Proverbs 18:21 NIV)

One of my all-time favorite movies is *The Help*, which is based on an award-winning book of the same name by Kathryn Stockett. In case you haven't seen this amazing film, here's the basic plot. *The Help* is about African American maids working for white households in Mississippi in the 1960s. The movie shows these maids working tirelessly, taking care of their own families in addition to the white families in the homes where they are employed. It was a time of bitter segregation. The maids, who were treated like worthless commodities, were often referred to as "the help," hence, the title of the book and movie.

Most days, these maids spent more quality time with their employers' children than the children's actual parents spent with them. The maids loved these kiddos like they were their own.

Aibileen (played by Viola Davis) takes care of Miss Elizabeth's house and her two-year-old daughter, Mae Mobley—a little girl who doesn't exactly fit in with her mama's perfect world. You see, Mae Mobley is a little chubby and not very well-behaved, much to her mother's embarrassment. Because Mae Mobley isn't a perfectly beautiful little girl, her mama often physically and verbally abuses her, and Aibileen can't stand it. So, she loves on Mae Mobley every day, speaking words of life to her.

She looks Mae Mobley in the eyes, smiles at her, and says, "You is kind; you is smart; you is important." And, then she has the little girl repeat those positive affirmations back to her.

On Aibileen's final day as she's leaving Miss Elizabeth's home, the little girl runs after her. And, Aibileen squats down, takes Mae Mobley's hands in her own one last time, and says: "You is kind; you is smart; you is important."

As that scene played out, I "ugly cried" in the theater. Such a powerful moment!

You see, Aibileen knew she couldn't be there for all of Mae Mobley's growing-up years, but she also knew she had planted those words of life in the little girl's heart. And, she hoped Mae Mobley would begin to walk in those truths—that she would be kind and smart and important—no matter what her mother said, or anyone else for that matter.

How about you? What are you saying to your loved ones? Are you speaking words of life into your family and friends? Are you taking every opportunity to tell them how important they are and how much you treasure them? Are you respecting them and celebrating their worth?

And, what are you saying about yourself? Do you say what the Word of God says about you, or are you constantly speaking negatively about yourself?

If you truly believe that you are precious to the Lord, that He has bought you at a great price, then you wouldn't say derogatory statements about yourself. Right?

Listen, if you've been talking bad about yourself, end that nonsense today. Start saying things like, "I am a child of the Most High God." "I am the apple of God's eye." "I am a daughter of the King of Kings!"

Know your worth! Change your talk, and it'll change your walk. All of a sudden, you'll hold your head a little higher and you'll stand a little taller, knowing that you are highly valued and greatly loved by the Creator of the universe. Hallelujah!

PLATINUM PROJECT

Sometimes we treat our faith like a commodity. We often find ourselves on our knees in times of trouble, but how often do we find ourselves on our knees when things are going right?

Sometimes we give ourselves too much credit, particularly when our needs are met. It can be difficult to develop a heart of gratitude for things that we take for granted, yet if we truly have a platinum faith, we can rest assured that God will of course provide for us.

What are some blessings that God has given that are easy to take for granted? I'm in an air-conditioned home tucked comfortably onto my bed as I type, a healthy supply of K-Cups and sweet cream a few feet away should I feel the urge to guzzle some caffeine. I've got worries and concerns, sure, but compared to many who are suffering and being persecuted, I'm safe, healthy, protected, and loved. And I don't thank God enough for those blessings until one of them is compromised.

One way to nurture a grateful heart is to practice. Author and speaker Stephanie L. Jones developed *The Giving Challenge*, which is all about taking forty days to focus on others. At the time of this printing, Stephanie is currently working on her next book, *The Gratitude Challenge*.

Find a way to participate in one of those challenges, or if you need a different idea, start a gratitude journal. Each night, write down at least one thing you are grateful for that day.

Over time, this record shows the blessings that we all too often forget about.

Because unlike tangible commodities that are bought and sold, God's love for us is something that He'll never trade.

He'll never let go.

Start today (and I will, too). Jot down some blessings. If

some worries come to mind, write them in the prayer journal we mentioned in a previous chapter. And as an extra step, if God brings someone to your mind, send them a text, e-mail, or Facebook message, or give them a call. Maybe God will use you to remind that person they are special, treasured, and worthy of love.

DISCUSSION QUESTIONS

1. Has there been a time when you have felt unloved and unwanted like Leah? How did you get through it?

2. The Bible tells us that we are precious, worthy, and wanted. Are you speaking words of life into your family, friends, and yourself? Do you say what the Word of God says about you, or are you constantly speaking negatively about yourself or others?

3. Set aside some time to journal. If God brings someone to mind, what are some ways you can remind that person that he or she is special, treasured, and worthy of love? How can you remind yourself?

Chapter 12

You Can Be Self-Controlled

Bethany

When you react, you let others control you. When you respond, you are in control.

Bodhi Sanders

Respond, don't react.

Seems simple enough. But flying off the handle is way too often the immediate reaction or letting a situation fester until you just can't take it anymore.

Responding to a situation takes thought, time, and clarity.

Reactions are often spontaneous.

Reactions are often embarrassing.

Sometimes I document my reactiveness. We've just moved from a rented townhouse into a three-bedroom split level as first-time homebuyers. This book is due in four days so I'm sitting at what we now refer to as "the old house" after letting the final move-out cleaning team come over and waiting for Stanley Steemer to arrive to do a last carpet cleaning. My company is launching a new product next week, I'm running two one-day conferences, and I was gone for two weeks out of this month.

And then Justin is called up on a mini-mission with less than twenty-four-hours notice. So instead of having a quiet day to write sans interruption aside from the two cleaning services, I arrived at the townhouse with the boys, who promptly dumped a bowl of water all over their carpet while supposedly washing the walls, then slapped each other with the wet towels.

Then we head to get the oil changed, another of my responsibilities this week since Justin's gone. Turns out they want $1000+ to replace hoses so the power steering won't leak, something Justin can do himself for much less.

And my patience meter begins to run out.

But reacting means there's not time for thoughtfulness. There's not time for prayer.

We are instructed to not be anxious, but it's always the things that make me anxious that I react to. Or rather, it's *when* I'm anxious that I react instead of taking the time to respond in an appropriate manner.

A Jesus-like manner.

The only time recorded in the Bible when Jesus had what we might refer to as a holy meltdown was when he overturned tables in the temple. This was righteous anger. Every other time Jesus interacted with others, His responses were always measured— even when they were reproving, as with the Pharisees. Because He is fully God, as well as fully human, His responses were always right.

His is the model we need to follow.

PLATINUM PROPERTY

One of the cool elements of platinum is that it belongs to the group of five metals that comprise the noble family. Noble metals don't *react* with other metals, that is, they don't combine with other chemicals to form a new compound.[1]

Platinum is happy being platinum and doesn't need to react when other metals are near it, which makes it a great candidate for use in pacemakers and other medical devices. Another characteristic of platinum is that because it is unreactive, it is a great metal to use as a catalyst: it can speed up a chemical reaction without changing in the process.[2]

Without changing in the process.

When life is spinning out of control, my faith doesn't always go to a noble platinum level. Often, I'll change with the situation, growing more nervous and anxious instead of trusting that God has everything under control.

The military reserves the right to call up Justin at a moment's notice. I have yet to not have a mild freak out ten minutes after he tells me he's leaving. The weight of all the items on his to-do list gets piled onto my shoulders, and I begin to crumple under the overwhelming reality of rearranging schedules and losing my partner for an undetermined amount of time.

The good news is, though, I'm getting better at responding to the situation calmly instead of reacting in panic and making quick changes to my schedule or canceling plans. Most of the time when I act this way, I regret it later. If I'd waited—simply *waited*—plans would have worked out better or I wouldn't have had to cancel plans at all.

Last summer I was supposed to speak at a writers conference that my company was partnering with. I'd never attended this particular event, and it was a dream come true to be on the faculty. Three days before I was scheduled to leave, Justin calls with news that he's in the lineup to be sent out on a mission in two days.

Ummm.

Just exactly who is supposed to stay home and take care of the kids?

Who is supposed to cancel their plans?

Me. That's who.

Because I'm the mom.

Because my job is not government sanctioned.

Because my life choices have to be fluid.

Disappointment knifed my heart and my stomach sank.

I held it together on the phone with Justin; after all, there's nothing he can do about it, and the last thing I want is for him to feel stressed on a mission.

But once I got off the phone, that's another story.

As I am a firstborn people-pleaser, the thought of disappointing everyone and not being able to attend the event, along with the stress of rearranging our schedule, changing all the plans, taking over all of Justin's responsibilities, and the emptiness that comes from missing him so much while he's gone, was just too much.

With the event just days away, I felt like I had to take care of the situation at that exact moment.

I felt out of control, so to regain the illusion of control, I sprang into action.

I called Michelle and burst into tears.

I called my mom. Tears.

I called the director of the writers conference.

I made arrangements to miss the event.

And then an hour later, I get a phone call from my husband. The mission supervisors decided to take only the first three guys on the list.

Justin was number four.

I'd freaked out for no reason and probably came across like an idiot to the director I was trying to impress.

Instead of stopping to pray, I let impulsiveness win.

Adrenaline flooded my veins, and I stressed my body unnecessarily. Where was the platinum faith? Where was the assurance that God had a plan?

In the midst of a perceived crisis, I wilted.

Crumbled.

Reacted.

Have you been there?

Have you ever felt completely out of control? It's hard to stop when the world feels like it's spinning around you. We grasp for any area of control even if it's not the best long-term decision.

James 1:19 says to let everyone be quick to listen and slow to speak. In other words, slow to respond.

So in the midst of chaos, let us pause, take deep breaths, and remember to be quick to listen for God's direction and slow to respond so that we can stay in control instead of letting the situation control us.

Live Brilliant: The Heat of the Moment

MICHELLE

Ever heard the quote, "We can't control what happens to us in life, but we can control how we respond"? That's really true. Circumstances are often out of our control, aren't they? That brings to mind another quote from "To a Mouse" by Robert Burns: "The best-laid schemes of mice and men/Go often askew." Can I get an amen?

June in Indiana is usually very mild—the perfect month for an outdoor wedding. Then again, it is Indiana, and the weather is very unpredictable. Still, when we were planning my oldest daughter's outdoor wedding, June 11, 2016, seemed like the perfect day to get married. We'd made all of the necessary arrangements in case of rain, but the weather forecast looked clear as we headed toward that special day. In fact, the weather every day the week before June 11 was absolutely gorgeous, even a little chilly at night. We were so excited!

Then, the very day of the wedding, things heated up, and when I say "things," I mean we heated up. It was 94 degrees without one sign of a breeze. We were on fire! Seriously, I've never been that hot before or since that day. As we sat on those stone benches beneath the scorching sun, I felt like a pizza on one of those baking stones I'd once purchased at a Pampered

Chef party. And, of course, we were wearing black because Abby's colors were black, champagne, and ivory. At one point, my sweet mother-in-law actually passed out during pictures.

We figured once the sun set, it would cool off and the evening breeze would carry us through the reception.

We were wrong.

It was still hot—possibly hotter.

I remember looking around the venue at all of the red faces and the paper fans moving at warp speed as people desperately tried to cool off, and I said to my husband, "People are so hot. What are we going to do?"

"We are going to enjoy every moment of this day," he said, "And drink a lot of water."

And, we did.

We were happy and hydrated.

Will Abby's and Micah's wedding go down in history as one of the hottest ceremonies ever?

It's possible.

But it was also one of the most special ceremonies ever.

We couldn't control or change the circumstances, but we could control how we responded. We joked about the heat, made sure everyone drank water, and relished in every vow, toast, and dance.

I learned a good lesson that day. Reacting—giving into the heat of the moment (literally)—wouldn't bring about the desired result. Panicking or getting angry about the weather wouldn't have changed anything for the better. Yes, having a mad fit probably would've felt good to my flesh for a moment, but

I would've regretted acting that way on my daughter's special day.

My mama always said, "When in doubt, choose peace."

That's what I did on June 11, 2016. I chose peace when the flowers wilted due to the heat. I chose peace when we couldn't find the flower girls' baskets. I chose peace when there was a bit of extended family drama brewing. I chose peace at every turn that day, and that's how we survived the hottest wedding day in history.

Looking back, what seemed like a big thing that day really doesn't seem too monumental today. In fact, the intense heat certainly made their wedding day memorable! (Sweat beads are forming above my lip just thinking about it!) So, I'm telling you today, choose peace. Don't react; respond. And, don't sweat it! (Unless its 94 degrees with no breeze—then you're allowed to sweat.)

INUIT RESPONSIVENESS

Not all cultures are quick to react instead of respond. Native to Alaska, Inuit families raise their children to control their emotions without timeouts and raising their voices. Instead, the Inuit utilize the power of storytelling.

They favor "oral stories passed down from one generation of Inuit to the next, designed to sculpt kids' behaviors in the moment."[3] According to Jean Briggs, who lived with the Inuit while studying their parenting style of responding instead of reacting, the Inuit view acting frustrated or getting upset as a symptom of childlike behavior and therefore culturally unacceptable.

The storytelling aspect of training children is not new, but the Inuit go a step farther and create what Briggs called "mini dramas." Parents repeatedly reenact the episode where children got upset and demonstrate the proper way to handle their response.

It's a much different parenting style than a Westernized one and, more so, different than how I respond to my kids. I raise my voice at my sons, so why am I surprised when they raise their voices at each other?

As a role model for my children, I don't think I'm doing a very good job in this area, considering my kids "rage quit" their video game battles when they think someone is cheating online (which is basically anytime my kids' avatar is killed).

I've got room for improvement here.

One of the ways I'm trying to do better is by speaking calmly and deepening my tone of voice instead of yelling. My mom's side of the family are avid dog lovers and used to raise dogs for different charitable programs. In fact, my aunt is now a dog breeder. They all know so much about training dogs for obedience and agility, with dozens of blue ribbons and trophies to prove it! A teensy bit of their knowledge has rubbed off, and one of the more fascinating conversations we've had is how raising dogs has similarities to raising children.

When my mom was in the agility ring and her dog made a mistake, nine times out of ten, it was my mom's fault. Either her body position was incorrect or she made the wrong motion. The dog was simply responding to what it thought my mom wanted it to do.

Family life is similar.

My kids often respond to my actions and mood, and a simple change in my tone or facial expression can swing the attitudes of my children. If I'm grumpy and yelling, those negative emotions cling to my boys' hearts, and they, in turn, begin to grump and yell at each other.

Another similarity goes back to the tone of voice. Dogs don't respond well to yelling, but using an authoritative and firm tone often does the trick. I've noticed that my boys respond better when I speak firmly and a little deeper than normal, as opposed to yelling, which in my case is higher pitched and sounds a bit out of control.

The third way I'm trying to be a better parent is to use story. Similar to the Inuit tradition, Jesus also told stories to get His point across. While we might assume that Jesus spoke in parables so that the masses that followed Him would be able to comprehend, Jesus spoke in parables specifically because they wouldn't.[4]

These parables are defined as earthly stories with heavenly meanings. When the disciples asked Jesus one time why He taught in parables (see Matthew 13:10), Jesus's answer is thought-provoking, even for us today:

> And he answered them, "To you it has been given to know the secrets of the kingdom of heaven, but to them it has not been given. For to the one who has, more will be given, and he will have an abundance, but from the one who has not, even what he has will be taken away. This is why I speak to them in parables, because seeing

they do not see, and hearing they do not hear, nor do they understand."

(Matthew 13:11-13 ESV)

Even though the Son of God was standing right before these people, many of them did not understand the truths that He was teaching them. Jesus then quotes from Isaiah before saying this to His disciples:

But blessed are your eyes, for they see, and your ears, for they hear. For truly, I say to you, many prophets and righteous people longed to see what you see, and did not see it, and to hear what you hear, and did not hear it.

(Matthew 13:16-17 ESV)

Stories are powerful, especially when told in the proper context that is specific for the audience. Inuit parents tell stories to teach their children particular lessons. Jesus told stories that pointed to God's love and to salvation.

As parents, coworkers, spouses, daughters, sisters, family, and friends, we can choose to respond to each other instead of reacting. Perhaps using story to share our feelings will slow down our emotions enough so that we can make a clear and solid point.

And perhaps by taking time to breathe and think, we'll build bridges in our relationships and continue to strengthen the bonds we have with each other.

PLATINUM PROMISE

We make bad decisions when we react. Just ask the red hairy guy who impulsively traded his birthright, the equivalent of two-thirds of his father's entire inheritance, for a bowl of stew. We characterize Esau with impulsiveness but I'm not convinced it's an accurate reflection of his character.

Esau was a hunter by trade. I've watched enough *Duck Dynasty* to know that hunting is not an impulsive man's game. And yet, the scene is set.

One person has something the other person wants and will do anything to get it.

Recently we drove into Macon, Missouri, and the aroma that permeated the windows of the car was mouth-watering. Consider that we were headed to lunch and it comes as no surprise that tummies were growling.

At first I thought the delicious smell was coming from homes where people were barbecuing in their backyards, or maybe it was coming from the restaurant on the corner. Instead, the smell got stronger as we turned onto the street where the ConAgra packaged food plant pumped its steam into the air.

The wonderful smells of meals being prepared only fueled my hunger.

Activity also fuels appetite. My kids are ravenous after they've been playing outside in the swimming pool; and with three growing boys, it's hard to keep enough food in the house. We can only imagine how starving Esau must have been after a full day of being in the fields:

> Once when Jacob was cooking stew, Esau came in from the field, and he was exhausted. And Esau said to Jacob, "Let me eat some of that red stew, for I am exhausted!" (Therefore his name was called Edom.) Jacob said, "Sell me your birthright now." Esau said, "I am about to die; of what use is a birthright to me?" Jacob said, "Swear to me now." So he swore to him and sold his birthright to Jacob. Then Jacob gave Esau bread and lentil stew, and he ate and drank and rose and went his way. Thus Esau despised his birthright. (Genesis 25:29-34 ESV)

I think Jacob was a jokester. His name literally means "deceiver," and I'm sure he'd played plenty of practical jokes on his twin brother. I'd bet money that Esau never expected to actually give up his birthright.

All Esau wanted was his meal, and there was no way for Jacob to actually receive his inheritance, so Esau agreed. And ate. And was deceived by not only his brother but also his mom. He lost his birthright. All for a bowl of stew. So many times I am Esau, willing to devalue the inheritance of God for something finite, which doesn't last and doesn't fill.

When I think about our faith in terms of being unreactive, unchanging, not conforming (or becoming a new compound when mixed with other chemicals), a particular verse in the Bible comes to mind.

And it just might be the most frightening verse I've ever read. E-V-E-R.

Second Timothy 4:3-4 states: "For the time will come when people will not put up with sound doctrine. Instead, to suit their own desires, they will gather around them a great number of teachers to say what their itching ears want to hear. They will turn their ears away from the truth and turn aside to myths" (NIV).

People won't put up with sound doctrine.

Put up with?

They'll turn their ears from truth to myth to suit what we want to hear.

Are we there?

Christianity isn't politically correct. Are we short-changing God's word to feed the itching ears of our social media audiences? Do we stick to noncontroversial topics so we don't have to take a stand?

Or worse, do we change our viewpoints depending on who we are around? Is some sin OK if we're with our close friends but not OK when we're in public?

Who do my itching ears listen to because I don't want to be faced with the truth over my own sin?

How many times do I silently applaud those willing to face the criticism and backlash from the opposing view while I sit comfortably behind my iPhone screen, safe from controversy?

And do I excuse this behavior by hiding behind Paul's declaration that he is all things to all people—he's weak to the people who are weak, becomes a Jew to the Jews, and so on—all to win people to God?

> *Though I am free and belong to no one, I have made myself a slave to everyone, to win as many as possible. To the Jews I became like a Jew, to win the Jews. To those under the law I became like one under the law (though I myself am not under the law), so as to win those under the law. To those not having the law I became like one not having the law (though I am not free from God's law but am under Christ's law), so as to win those not having the law. To the weak I became weak, to win the weak. I have become all things to all people so that by all possible means I might save some. I do all this for the sake of the gospel, that I may share in its blessings.*
> (1 Corinthians 9:19-23 NIV)

Paul's motive is pure, and he remains steadfast and strong in his beliefs.

Do we?

Paul's faith is platinum: fused to the truths of God's Word; and he does not depart from it.

So how do we hold on to that platinum faith and not let go?

PLATINUM PROJECT

Platinum faith means we respond to situations in a manner worthy of our title as daughters of the King.

We control our response instead of letting the situation control us.

When faced with a situation that is upsetting, simply take a break, step back, and evaluate the options. Then make a decision.

This works with minor decisions, too, like where to put the tall IKEA bookshelf when you realize it's not going to fit where you think it should.

I was sold on having a new vanity set and scoured Pinterest until I found four options. I let Justin pick his favorite, and boom—we're off to the races. But the table was too long, and I wasn't going to be able to frame the vanity with these beautiful thin bookshelves that would mirror the floor-to-ceiling windows.

Reaction: move the bookcase to a different part of the room and have Justin return the second bookcase.

Something amazing happened though. When I woke up the next morning, I realized how disappointed I was to not have the bookcases frame the area. All of a sudden it hit me—just get a smaller table.

Everything started fitting into place.

We moved the long table downstairs into my office (where we were about to purchase a long table anyway) and moved the smaller table that currently was in our kitchen nook area upstairs.

Perfection! And room to spare.

While furniture is a minor thing compared to serious and sometimes life-threatening situations, it made me realize how often I default into "fix it and move on" mode instead of giving things time. I'm always rushing and that's no way to live.

Whatever "furniture moment" you're dealing with right now, I suggest taking time if possible. Isaiah 40:31 says, "But they who wait for the LORD shall renew their strength" (ESV). Sometimes the wait is long and sometimes makes us weary, but when we react instead of respond, we don't make allowance for God to really work in our hearts.

Why not sit at His feet today, perhaps with an extra few minutes in silent prayer? Our Heavenly Father is always listening, always ready, and always there.

Pray with me.

Dear God, give us grace and patience to deal with situations, both big and small, as they arise. Help us to rest in Your peace and not default to a stress-mode that leads to ungodliness. Thank you for being the amazing Father that You are. We love You and praise You. In Jesus's name, Amen.

DISCUSSION QUESTIONS

1. In the New Testament, Paul's motive is pure, and he remains steadfast and strong in his beliefs. Do you cling to the truths of God's Word like Paul did, or do you find yourself departing from it based on your situation?

2. Platinum doesn't change when there's a chemical reaction. It responds but doesn't react. When you're faced with a challenging or uncomfortable circumstance, do you react out of your emotions or do you calmly think through the situation and respond in a mature fashion?

3. Platinum faith means we control our emotions and, thereby, our responses instead of letting the situations control us. What are some practical things you can do to respond to a disturbing situation rather than overreacting or acting immaturely?

CHAPTER 13

You Are Authentic

MICHELLE

*When we live authenticity instead of do authenticity,
not only will we have a greater influence and credibility
as salt and light, but God will be glorified through who
we are.*

Paul Sohn

What does it mean to be authentic?

Dictionary.com defines *authentic* as "not false or copied; genuine; real."[1]

Let's face it—nobody likes a fake. And, I'm not talking about coloring your hair or getting a spray tan, because I'm guilty of both of those. I'm talking about the fake personas we don, the masks we wear, so the whole world will think we've got it all together when in reality, we are the definition of a "hot mess."

I know I've been guilty of this at various times in my life. For example, one Sunday morning when the girls were little, we were all headed to church when fighting broke out in the backseat. Allyson threw her sippy cup at Abby, showering her with sticky apple juice, which made Abby retaliate by throwing her container of "fishy crackers" back at her sister. It was a blur of airborne fish and juice droplets, followed by lots of yelling and crying. All of the stress of the backseat brawl caused my usually calm hubby to lash out at me for no reason, so I felt the need to yell right back. As we pulled into the church parking lot, the fighting continued, even louder. But the minute we opened the doors to our Ford Explorer, we put on our masks—Sal and Sylvia Super Christian. As we walked into church, holding hands, one of the church greeters said, "Welcome, how are you today?"

"Oh, I'm blessed, Sister," I responded, smiling the teethiest grin I could muster. Of course, inside I was wounded because Jeff had yelled; I was mad at myself for participating in the strife. And, I was aggravated at the girls for behaving so badly.

Authentic?

Not even close.

Maybe you can relate.

I think that's why most people love to hear evangelist Joyce Meyer preach because she's so real. She doesn't mind pulling back the "false veil of perfection" and giving you a glimpse into her real world—a world where she doesn't always get it right. That makes her likeable, believable, and authentic.

In a world that's caught up in branding and projecting the perfect persona on all social media platforms, it's becoming more and more difficult to be real. I mean, how many of us post a picture of our piles of clothes on the floor in the laundry room or the dirty dishes in the sink from last night's dinner? Very few, I'd say, if any. No, we pose in our favorite leopard print chair, sipping coffee from a cool mug we found on sale at Target, and take a selfie in the one area of our house that is actually free from clutter, writing something like: Loving my life "a latte" in my leopard chair. #homedecor #lovemylife

Our hashtags should actually read: #therestofmyhouseisin totalchaos #Ihavenotsleptinthreedays #liarliarpantsonfire.

Listen, I'm all for putting your best foot forward and not sharing your "dirty laundry" on social media platforms—both figuratively and literally—but here's my point. We need to be authentic in real life and online. You know why? Because when we are, we give others permission to be real, too. We can drop all the facades and simply be who we are, who God created us to be, flaws and all.

You've probably heard the old adage (that's been loosely attributed to Abraham Lincoln) that says: "You can fool all the people some of the time and some of the people all the time, but you cannot fool all the people all the time."

That's true.

You know what else is true?

You can't fool yourself *any* of the time. You may put on a smile and transform into "Sylvia Super Christian" like I did that morning at church, but you'll be miserable on the inside until God transforms your heart. It's so much better to be real—with people, with yourself, and with God. He knows everything anyway.

But, until we can be real with God; until we can confess our sins, tell Him our weaknesses, share with Him our dreams; until we can allow God to know every little part of our lives; until we can trust Him fully with the good, the bad, and the ugly parts of our hearts, we can't fully walk in platinum faith.

Do you trust Him today?

PLATINUM PROPERTY

Just like it's sometimes easy to fool others, never letting them see the authentic you, it's also easy to *be fooled* by good fakes. Take faux designer handbags, for example. They can look identical to the real ones, except to the trained eye, which will spot a difference in the stitching or a tiny discrepancy in the positioning of the label. And, a high-quality cubic zirconia sometimes has more sparkle and vibrance than an actual diamond! Only a jeweler can tell the difference with a special magnifying tool. Likewise, white gold and sterling silver can look a lot like platinum in certain circumstances—especially if you aren't really familiar with the various precious white metals. But, there are a few markers to help you determine which is platinum and which is sterling and white gold. First off, platinum is harder, heavier, and shiner than white gold and sterling silver. Also, white gold will turn a little yellow as it ages, and silver will tarnish. Platinum won't do either. Lastly, if you find a piece of jewelry featuring an expensive gemstone, you can immediately rule out silver, narrowing it down to platinum or white gold. Usually, white gold will have a *k* alongside a number stamped on it, signifying karat weight, and platinum will have *pt* or *plat* imprinted on it somewhere.

But, even with those markers, it's still sometimes difficult to differentiate between all of the white metals, even when you're looking really hard.[2]

PLATINUM PROMISE

Not long ago, I was browsing in a quaint little jewelry store, admiring a platinum piece, and the woman behind the counter shared a story with me about a particular platinum necklace that one of her customers had recently inherited.

It seems this woman's mother-in-law had recently died and her two sisters-in-law had claimed all of the valuable pieces of jewelry for themselves, leaving her only the costume pieces. She understood, of course, because her husband obviously wasn't planning on wearing any of his late mother's jewelry, but still she was hoping she might end up with one nice piece for which to remember her mother-in-law. Saddened by how her sisters-in-law had handled all of the dividing of the assets, including the jewelry, this woman didn't even go through the costume pieces for several months. Then one afternoon, she sorted through each drawer of the jewelry box, remembering her mother-in-law wearing several of the pieces. All of the jewelry sort of blended together in a sea of rhinestones and tarnished metal.

Except for one necklace.

It was definitely old and in need of a deep cleaning, but it was heavier than all of the other pieces. She brought the necklace into a jeweler several towns over from where she lived, to find out if the necklace had any value, other than sentimental. Turns out, it was platinum! And, not just any platinum necklace; it was a custom piece worth thousands of dollars! The jeweler gently cleaned the very special necklace, revealing its shiny white metal and intricate design work that had been hidden by all of the grime.

The woman and the jeweler were amazed by its beauty.

Obviously, the sisters had passed over the platinum stunner because the piece looked like a silver-plated necklace at best. It didn't appear to be worth very much. But it was quite valuable— more valuable than all of the other pieces of jewelry put together. It just took a master jeweler to verify its identity and worth.

Well, guess what? It's the same way with God. We may be fooled but He is not. He has always been able to discern fake faith, and He was quick to call them on it (see Matthew 23:16-17 and Matthew 23:33).

Let's look at one passage of these counterfeit faith-ers called Pharisees:

> *And as He spoke, a certain Pharisee asked Him to dine with him. So He went in and sat down to eat. When the Pharisee saw it, he marveled that He had not first washed before dinner. Then the Lord said to him, "Now you Pharisees make the outside of the cup and dish clean, but your inward part is full of greed and wickedness. Foolish ones! Did not He who made the outside make the inside also? But rather give alms of such things as you have; then indeed all things are clean to you.*
>
> *"But woe to you Pharisees! For you tithe mint and rue and all manner of herbs, and pass by justice and the love of God. These you ought to have done, without leaving the others undone. Woe to you Pharisees! For you love the best seats in the synagogues and greetings in the marketplaces. Woe to you, scribes and Pharisees, hypocrites! For you are like graves which are not seen, and the men who walk over them are not aware of them."*
>
> *(Luke 11:37-44 NKJV)*

He was saying, "You do all of these things to impress others, faking your way through life, but I'm not impressed because I see you for who you really are—posers and wicked hypocrites!" If the Pharisees would have had access to social media, you can bet they would've been posting selfies while sitting in the best seats in the synagogue, hash-tagging like there was no tomorrow: #bestseatin thehouse #yousowannnabeme #tithingismylife.

God wasn't impressed with the Pharisees back then, and He's not impressed with the modern-day Pharisees, either. The Word says that men and God judge differently. First Samuel 16:7b says, "The LORD does not look at the things people look at. People look at the outward appearance, but the LORD looks at the heart" (NIV). We can't see behind the mask, but God can. He stares straight into the heart of every person.

But it's not always just the high-and-mighty, self-righteous types who are inauthentic where their faith walk is concerned. It's also the ones who put their faith in themselves, their accomplishments, and their material things, rather than putting their faith in God.

We can see that here in the story of the rich young ruler:

> And someone came to Him and said, "Teacher, what good thing shall I do that I may obtain eternal life?" And He said to him, "Why are you asking Me about what is good? There is only One who is good; but if you wish to enter into life, keep the commandments." Then he said to Him, "Which ones?" And Jesus said, "YOU SHALL NOT COMMIT MURDER; YOU SHALL NOT COMMIT ADULTERY; YOU SHALL NOT STEAL; YOU SHALL NOT BEAR FALSE WITNESS; HONOR YOUR FATHER AND MOTHER; and YOU SHALL LOVE YOUR NEIGHBOR AS YOURSELF." The young man said to Him, "All these things I have kept; what am I still lacking?" Jesus said to him, "If you wish to be complete, go and sell your possessions and give to the poor, and you will have treasure in heaven; and come, follow Me." But when the young man heard this statement, he went away grieving; for he was one who owned much property.
>
> And Jesus said to His disciples, "Truly I say to you, it is hard for a rich man to enter the kingdom of heaven. Again I say to you, it is easier for a camel to go through the

eye of a needle, than for a rich man to enter the kingdom of God." (Matthew 19:16-24 NASB)

You see, the man who is referred to as "the rich young ruler" had counterfeit or faux faith. It wasn't his riches that kept him from possessing real, authentic, platinum faith; it was his fear that Jesus wouldn't be enough. This young ruler's faith was in himself and what he had accumulated. He was afraid of losing that money, that status, and that security. He wasn't a bad man. He had kept all the other commandments since he was a boy, but he wasn't "all in." Platinum faith means going all in—nothing withheld—with the right heart.

Live Brilliant:
Imposter Syndrome

BETHANY

Imposter syndrome is a psychological condition in which people doubt their abilities and achievements and feel like frauds.

Like counterfeits.

The underlying issue is that their success is due to luck instead of their talents or qualifications.[3] In 2018, *Time* magazine did an article on the truth behind imposter syndrome and featured Valerie Young, an expert on imposter syndrome.

Young categorized patterns that are typical of people struggling with imposter syndrome, including people who are perfectionists, experts, "natural geniuses," soloists, and supermen and superwomen. She says, "The goal is not to never feel like an impostor. The goal for me is to give [people] the tools and the insight and information to talk themselves down faster. They can still have an impostor moment, but not an impostor life."[4]

I've felt this way when it comes to social media and marketing. Because I'm finishing my master's degree in communications, focusing specifically on marketing and PR, the weight of being able to pull off the marketing side of my businesses and my brand as an author feels so heavy.

The more I learn, the more I know what I *don't*

know, and the imposter syndrome feels very, very real.

Have you ever felt this way?

Has the pressure to succeed ever made you feel sick to your stomach? Like you couldn't breathe? Like you don't deserve to take a break or rest because someone thinks you should be working harder?

Is this pressure coming from others?

Is it coming from you?

Come with me, my fellow imposter syndrome sufferers, and let's see what God says.

"For we are God's handiwork, created in Christ Jesus to do good works, which God prepared in advance for us to do" (Ephesians 2:10 NIV).

We are God's handiwork.

Created in Christ Jesus.

To do good works.

Which God prepared in advance for us to do.

When the task seems overwhelming, when the pressure gets to be too much, let's remember that God created us for these good works. He gets the glory. It's not about us and our achievements but about doing our best. Let's temper that knowledge with this verse: "Let your light shine before others, that they may see your good deeds and glorify your Father in heaven" (Matthew 5:16 NIV).

It's all for His glory so when we feel like we can't, let's remember that we are God's children, His creation, and we are enough.

WALK IN FAITH

Our pastor once said that true faith is not the end but the means. God is the end. I thought that was really good. True faith—platinum faith—knows no limits because platinum faith is rooted in the King of all Kings! Counterfeit faith, sometimes referred to as humanism, is limited to human beings. It never goes beyond what a person can dream and do on his or her own.

John 6:63 says, "Human effort accomplishes nothing" (NLT). That's why we must operate beyond ourselves.

For us to truly walk in platinum faith, God must be involved in every step we take because He knows the end result; He knows the way; and He will help us get there. The prophet Jeremiah understood what it meant to walk in platinum faith, and he also knew that humanism would lead to destruction. In fact, Jeremiah was known for calling out false prophets as posers and fakes. He understood that apart from God, we can do nothing. "I know, LORD, that our lives are not our own. We are not able to plan our own course" (Jeremiah 10:23 NLT).

Bottom line?

We need God.

Being inauthentic or having fake faith can only take us so far. Eventually, someone will see us for what we really are—a piece of tarnished silver or yellowing white gold—and our "Sylvia Super Christian" cover will be blown. So, quit trying to fake your way through life, and get real with God today. Relying on yourself can only take you so far, but fully trusting in Him can take you places you haven't even imagined!

PLATINUM PROJECT

You may say, "That sounds great, Michelle, but I don't feel like I have real faith, and I'm quite certain I don't have platinum faith. Most days, I feel like I'm not a strong enough Christian to do anything much for God."

Truth is, most of us don't feel like we have platinum faith every single day. Most of us feel like posers, faking our way through faith circles, trying to hide the truth—that we are in need of Almighty God to do a heart transformation on us.

So, let's get real with God today. Let's rip off those masks and bask in His presence. Pray with me: "We praise You, God, for all that You've done for us. Help us, Father, to trust You more and have that all-in kind of faith. Give me the courage, Lord, to let people see me, the real me, and let that real me point back to You. Thank You, Lord. In Your Son's Mighty Name, Amen."

Your platinum project this week is simply to keep a journal of all the times you feel like you're crossing over into inauthentic land, and then reflect on those instances during your quiet time with God. Ask Him to show you why you felt the need to fake it rather than show your true self. As you get to know the real you—the transformed you, the you that's becoming more Christ-like every day—you'll like "Sylvia Super Christian" less and your true self more.

Now, go forth and be courageously authentic.

DISCUSSION QUESTIONS

1. In Matthew, we read about "the rich young ruler" who had counterfeit faith. It wasn't his riches that kept him from possessing authentic faith; it was his fear that Jesus wouldn't be enough. Are there parts of your life that you have not yet surrendered to Jesus?

2. Imposter syndrome is a psychological condition in which people doubt their abilities and achievements and feel like frauds. Have you ever felt this way and focused on your own shortcomings? If so, what was the end result?

3. The text tells us that true faith is not the end but the means. God is the end. For us to have authentic faith, God must be involved in every step. What are some steps you can take toward having authentic faith?

CHAPTER 14

Rainbow Kisses and Silver-Dime Hugs

BETHANY

We only need to open our eyes to see the gifts that abound all around us. These are the simple joys in life.

Genevieve Gerard

I would have been a manna hoarder.

In my mind they taste like the Chick-fil-A's sweet honey-brushed breakfast Chick-n-Minis bread that encapsulates the nuggets.

The Israelites whining about wandering in the desert is one of the stories in Scripture that is a bit mind-boggling. God delivered them out of bondage and ushered them to safety in the most miraculous of ways. Imagine sweeping your fingertips across the wall of Red Sea water as you walk on dusty silt that's never seen the light of day.

Imagine being face-to-face with sea life staring out at you as you trek through a passage no person was ever meant to impose upon.

Imagine watching your enemies drown before your very eyes as your God takes His vengeance.

And then imagine questioning that same God when the Promised Land wasn't right around the corner.

And even though I've never touched the bottom of the sea nor glimpsed the depths of the Egyptians' watery grave, I've witnessed God's miraculous work in my life and the lives of my friends and family. I've prayed for a friend to be spared open heart surgery when her heart was working at less than half its capacity. God by His awesome power allowed her to need only a stint and an outpatient procedure.

We serve a big God.

Yet I whine when I have to wait even though my waiting experience includes air conditioning, fast food, and Amazon Prime.

And still, God loves us when we fail to trust.

Have you ever asked God for a sign? Have you ever needed Him to just *show* you the path you needed to take?

When I find myself wishing for a tangible answer, I think about the scene in *Indiana Jones and the Last Crusade* where Harrison Ford is on his quest for the Holy Grail. He is on one side of a canyon, with a door on the opposite side. Based on his clues to find the grail, he needs to take a leap of faith, but the ground below is oh-so-far away.

Spoiler alert: With no other options, he takes a step off the cliff, only to find a bridge that was camouflaged to look like the canyon.

The step of faith.

The Bible says we walk by faith, not by sight (see 2 Corinthians 2:5-7). So is it wrong to ask our Heavenly Father for an answer that isn't invisible? Can we have a platinum faith if we need a sign?

If we look at the Scriptures, I believe that answer is yes.

PLATINUM PROMISE

God bestows evidence of His faithfulness for us in tangible ways. Gideon fleeced God, and God answered. Moses asked for manna, and God provided. It's not beyond the realm of possibility to imagine that the unchanging God of Abraham would also provide us with a physical means of His love, mercy, and glory.

God even shows Himself when we don't have platinum faith. The Israelites had just witnessed the parting of the Red Sea and then groaned in the desert. How could they have such little faith? We are aghast at their lack of remembrance of what God could do. Would He really leave them to starve after that great rescue?

Because we can't seem to remember God's amazing grace when something bad happens.

Sometimes these tangible reminders come in the form of God's love whispers. We serve the same God who rescued Noah and his family from worldwide destruction.

Considering that Noah lost every friend and relative, with the exception of his wife and kids, in the flood, it's safe to say that Noah's faith was at a platinum level. He *knew* God saved him specifically, and yet in that time, even though Scripture doesn't mention this, the time on the ark had to be a time of mourning.

This was a new era. A fresh start. A literal brand-new world.

The floodwaters receded and the earth began to settle after the most catastrophic event this planet has ever known. After witnessing this destruction, wouldn't it make sense that Noah would consider that God might do this again?

But we serve a loving Father who meets us where we are.

God could have told Noah His plan to not flood the earth. I mean, He told Noah how to build the ark to exact proportions, but instead, God went a step further.

It's recorded in Genesis 9:17 that God visually displays His promise, His covenant. In a symbolic gesture, God places a *qešet* in the sky, a Hebrew word for "weapon." We see this word also used in conjunction with David's bestie Jonathan's bow, with Jehu shooting Joram in 2 Kings, and with God Himself in Psalm 7:12 where it says that God will make Himself ready with the bow if man does not repent.

But a bow has a straight piece, the bowstring, which is where the arrows are placed. Picture Katniss Everdeen from the young-adult dystopian best seller *The Hunger Games*. Her skill with a bow and arrow saves her life on multiple occasions.

For Katniss, the bow is a symbol of protection.

For Noah, it's a symbol of peace.

For us, the *qešet* is a symbol of God's promise to never destroy the earth again by water, but this *qešet*, this bow, is missing the bowstring.

Disarmed.

Neutralized.

A symbol resting on clouds of a covenant between our Creator and the created.

Our God and His people.

Our Father and His children.

The rainbow is still a reminder to us of God's great mercy.

To Michelle, it's also a reminder of the warmth and gentleness of her parents.

RAINBOW KISSES

Michelle's father, sweet Walter Medlock, one of the finest men ever to walk this earth, passed away after fighting sickness and multiple strokes. She left the rehabilitation center drained and depleted after he took his final breaths.

It was early May, not too hot, and there had been a soft rain. The gray sky matched Michelle's mood as she drove down the highway between Decatur and Fort Worth with her two little girls tucked into the backseat.

As she drove, a brilliant double rainbow materialized and covered the sky in front of them.

"Look, mommy!" Abby cried out from the backseat. "Papaw has a rainbow for Ally and a rainbow for me!" In Abby's mind, that rainbow was a promise from God that she would see their papaw again.

I love that God uses the visual and tangible to show His love to us.

How does God reveal Himself to you? Is it through other Christians? Is it in the words of a song that comes on the radio at just the right moment? Is it in the words of a sermon that touch on a topic you've been struggling with that very week? Is it through a million things that nonbelievers would chalk up to mere coincidence?

In the Bible, we see an example where a man asked specifically for an answer, for confirmation, and God responded.

FLEECED

When it comes to asking God to give us a sign, I have mixed feelings. In the Old Testament, we see time after time where God was questioned but didn't respond in a negative way. In fact, sometimes He showed Himself in the exact manner the person requested.

Gideon may be one of the more popular examples of when someone asks God for a sign. The Israelites were going to wage an epic battle, and Gideon needed to be absolutely sure he was following God's will and not his own. He asks God to prove that it was God answering him. Gideon made a request that defied the laws of nature:

> Then Gideon said to God, "If you will save Israel by my hand, as you have said, behold, I am laying a fleece of wool on the threshing floor. If there is dew on the fleece alone, and it is dry on all the ground, then I shall know that you will save Israel by my hand, as you have said." And it was so. When he rose early next morning and squeezed the fleece, he wrung enough dew from the fleece to fill a bowl with water. (Judges 6:36-38 ESV)

The super interesting part comes next because basically Gideon's at a crossroads. God complied and let the wool be so wet that the dew droplets filled a bowl when he squeezed it out and the ground around the fleece was dry.

Doesn't take a rocket scientist to see that Gideon's prayer was answered in the exact manner that it was requested.

Furthermore, have you ever squeezed water out of a fabric? When our air conditioner froze then melted all over the carpets upstairs, it took several towels to sop up the water that had thoroughly soaked the floor.

According to MacLaren's expositions, Gideon's

> petition for a sign was not the voice of unbelief or of doubt or of presumption, but in it spoke real, though struggling faith, seeking to be confirmed. Therefore it was not regarded by God as a sin. When a "wicked and adulterous generation asked for a sign," no sign was given it, but when faith asks for one to help it to grasp God's hand, and to go on His warfare in His strength and as His instrument, it does not ask in vain.[1]

> *Then Gideon said to God, "Let not your anger burn against me; let me speak just once more. Please let me test just once more with the fleece. Please let it be dry on the fleece only, and on all the ground let there be dew." And God did so that night; and it was dry on the fleece only, and on all the ground there was dew.*
>
> *(Judges 6:39-40 ESV)*

God demonstrated His power and shows us how the relationship between created and Creator is intimate. Not only was God's glory revealed but also God honored Gideon by complying to his request.

SILVER-DIME HUGS

Several years ago, my aunt on my mom's side found a dime outside on the ground. As she pocketed it, she commented that her dad, my Pappa, would always leave dimes for her to find. He'd empty his pockets and place a dime on top of a book that she was reading or at her seat at the table. It was their special thing. Whenever she saw one, she thought of him. And sometimes she saw dimes in the oddest of places, like in a hotel sink, the dressing room at her tailor's, and randomly in drawers at work (she doesn't use cash or change).

Another time, she was in the shower and spotted a lonely solitary dime in the corner where the tub met the tile wall.

She lived alone.

Every time I saw a dime on the ground, I thought of my aunt and my Pappa.

Until my grandma was in her final days of life.

About three weeks before her death, I started finding dimes in strange places. There would be a dime in the middle of the back-seat car mat or in a purse that had been carefully emptied out (with no other change beside it). The occurrences started happening so frequently that I took photos of each one and started keeping the dimes in a special place.

The craziest instance was after we'd moved to Mississippi for Justin's air force school. The apartment we'd rented in Tampa came with a washer and dryer so we needed to buy one for the house we were renting in Biloxi.

I searched on Facebook marketplace and asked around in a couple of online Facebook yard-sale groups. In the military-wives group, a lady reached out to me and said that she had an extra set, but they were rusted and ugly and needed a heating sensor.

Oh—and we could have them for free. Delivery included.

Lucky for me my husband is a Mr. Fix-it, and this lady happened to live in our neighborhood.

We unloaded the set off this nice couple's truck, shared a few stories about why they were at the base and where they were going next, and we promised to get together for a barbeque one day.

Justin ordered the heating part off of Amazon and two days later started fixing the dryer. The heat worked, but there was a strange rattling sound.

So Justin took the dryer apart again.

Do you see where I'm going with this?

"Babe," he said, walking into the kitchen a few minutes later. "You'll never guess what was making the sound in the dryer."

And he held up the smoothest, thinnest, most worn dime I'd ever seen in my life.

God's provision.

God's protection.

God's assurance to me—oh me of such little faith—that this move was the right step. That we were doing what God called us to do even though it was hard. Even though money was tight. Even though it felt crazy.

God gave me mercy when I didn't deserve it, and He gave me renewed hope through a tiny piece of metal.

A silver-dime hug.

And still, God continues to amaze me. I spoke at a women's event last week at a Christian college. Truth be told, I'd been speaking at writers events so often I was worried about speaking again to a church group. Understandably, I drove my mom and sister crazy with my neurosis and constant anxiety.

Before I spoke, I sat backstage in this cute, comfy lounge area, separated from the stage by a thick, heavy black curtain.

I sank into the couch to get my bearings and take a few deep breaths before it was my turn.

Would the ladies respond to my message?

Had I prepared enough?

Would I make it through my second point without crying?

As I pondered all these things, I happened to look down.

There on the coffee table, resting lightly on the weathered paperback Bible, was a shiny silver dime.

Live Brilliant:
God of the Promise

MICHELLE

I love everything about rainbows. As Bethany shared, rainbows have had significant meaning in my family's life since the passing of my father in 2004 and the appearance of the double rainbow stretching over that Texas highway.

Because rainbows have become so special to me personally, I spent a great deal of time researching them. And, one thing I discovered about rainbows is that there are seven common colors we can see with the naked eye, and they're always in the same order: red, orange, yellow, green, blue, indigo, and violet.[2]

Seven colors.

Seven—God's perfect number.

Coincidence? I think not.

So, the rainbow signifies not only God's promise to us but also His perfect promise.

His platinum promise.

That's why no matter what I'm facing in life, I know I can trust God. He didn't fail Noah. He's never failed me, and He won't fail you, either. Our Lord is trustworthy in all His promises and faithful in all He does.

Hebrews 10:23 says, "Let us hold fast the confession of *our* hope without wavering, for He who promised *is* faithful" (NKJV).

Just like that famous worship song says, He is the God of the promise.

Amen.

REMINDERS TO PRAY

A dear sweet friend of ours let us stay in her home for a week to work on this book. Her house provided a calm respite where we could be on our own schedule and work at our own pace. Michelle and I mentioned to her about the rainbows and dimes chapter in one of our conversations.

A week later, I heard from her.

"Every time I see a dime, it's a reminder to pray for you," she said. I can't express how truly humbled and so loved I felt when she said that.

And I love that dimes remind her to pray because similarly, when I see a rainbow, I think of God's promise to us, but I also see it as a reminder to stop and pray for Michelle.

These reminders are not coincidence. I believe the Holy Spirit prompts us and nudges us to pray for each other. The next time someone comes to your heart or to your mind, stop for a second, pray for them, and if it makes sense for your situation, maybe send them a text or jot a quick note. There have been so many times people have shared that they were praying for me and I just tilt my head to the sky and say, "Thank you, Father," because He knew what I was going through even if those people didn't. And I'm sure that it was His nudge that prompted their prayers, which I desperately needed.

We need to pray for each other. And as we close this book, we continue to pray for each other and also for you, dear reader, for your journey on this road to a Platinum Faith.

DISCUSSION QUESTIONS

1. God gives evidence of His faithfulness in tangible ways. Moses asked for manna, and God provided. The rainbow still reminds us of God's great mercy. How does God reveal Himself to you?

2. Gideon's "petition for a sign" was not the voice of unbelief or of doubt or of presumption, but in it spoke real, though struggling, faith, seeking to be confirmed. Has there been a time in your life when you asked God for a sign? How did He answer?

3. Set aside some time for reflection. What are some ways that you have been reassured of God's love in the past? How has that reassurance given you the encouragement to continue in your faith journey?

Conclusion

BETHANY

Never be afraid to trust an unknown future to a known God.

Corrie Ten Boom

Writing this book was one of the hardest things Michelle and I had to do. We shared stories we've never shared.

Cried tears we thought had been dried long ago.

So many times we'd text or call each other. "Why are we having to live each chapter as we write it?" Michelle said once.

We don't know.

Coming up with the platinum properties was easy.

Applying those properties with faith is much harder. We realized that we don't have platinum faith, but we're developing it; God is still working out good works in us even though we all too often miss the mark.

But the God we serve meets us where we are and journeys with us as we strive toward being more Christlike every day.

We hope you felt like you were on a journey, too. And yet, here we all stand on this side of the page. Stronger for where we've been and eager for the future. Our prayer for you (and for us) as we apply these characteristics of platinum to our faith is this:

May we have a faith that is bold, easily shaped, resistant to corruption and evil, untarnished, reflective of God's love, valuable, precious, special, and rare. And may we always look for tangible reminders of God's love for us.

Amen.

Prayer of Salvation

Father, it's written in Your Word that if I confess Jesus is Lord and believe in my heart that You have raised Him from the dead, I shall be saved.

Therefore, Father, I confess that Jesus is my Lord, and I make Him Lord of my life right now. I believe in my heart that Jesus died on the cross for my sins and that You raised Him from the dead. I repent for my past sins, and I thank You for forgiving me. I praise You, Father God, that I am a new creation from this moment forward. Old things have passed away; now all things become new. I love You, and I'm so grateful that You're my God. I pray all of this in the Mighty Name of Jesus. Amen.

Acknowledgments

Together, we'd like to say a big thanks to some people who were our cheerleaders and champions during our "Platinum Faith" journey:

Jeff Adams and Justin Jett—You are the best husbands ever. You make it possible for us to follow our dreams.

Cyle Young—We are so thankful to have you not only as our agent but also as our friend. You and Patty are like family, and we can't imagine doing life without you guys. #IllCallTheCops #YoureNotTheBossofMe! Haha!

Karen Longino—Thanks for believing in us and this project. Your trust and faith propelled this idea into a full-fledged brand. We're so thankful for that Catalyst meeting! Talk about divine appointments.

Joyce Glass—You are the answer to our PlatLit prayers. We could never have handled #allthestuff without you. We thank God for you every day!

To our prayer partners—We couldn't have done this without you. Truly.

Pat Bolton—Thank you for the use of your beautiful cabin and for your continued encouragement.

Jan Powell—You are such a blessing! Thanks for being a

lifesaver! Your hospitality, help, and encouragement have been invaluable to us. We still owe you a key!

Britt and Becca Mooney—Thanks for letting us stay at your house so that we could attend Catalyst in 2018. That Catalyst connection made this book possible. You and your precious family played a part in all of this, so thank you.

To the team at Abingdon—Thanks for all the editing, feedback, and support.

To all our friends—Thank you for the encouragement and prayers. You kept us going!

FROM MICHELLE

Jeff, Abby, and Ally, thanks for always supporting me in my calling to write, and thanks for encouraging me to continue when I start having feelings of self-doubt. I love you so much. I truly couldn't do what I do without you guys. And, Jeffrey, thanks especially to you for all of the Polar Pop deliveries and unconditional love. You're so good to me. Love you more.

I also want to thank Eva Marie Everson, Wendy Lanier, Angie McCullough, and Cecil Stokes. Thanks for being my sounding boards, brainstorming buddies, and friends I can always count on—no matter what. All of you shine so brightly for Jesus, I'm thankful for each one of you.

Oh, and I have to thank Ashley Kirby Jones, my social media and project manager person, but also my sweet and funny friend. Thanks for keeping "all things Michelle" in order. The Lord knew I needed a keeper. Thank goodness He sent you! I cannot thank you enough for all you do for me.

I especially want to thank Victoria Osteen for writing our foreword, and simply for being my longtime friend. You and Joel and your ministry have made such a difference in my life and the lives of so many others. You guys are a shining example of platinum faith. Thanks for all you do for the kingdom of God.

To Martie—my sister in the natural and in the Lord—thanks for being a pillar of faith for our family. Your dedication to the Lord is inspiring.

To Bethany—my little sister, my coauthor, business partner, and partner-in-crime—you are the moon to my sun. I seriously love you!!!! God must have known I needed a little sister when He allowed us to meet all those years ago at the Florida Christian Writers Conference. I am grateful to have shared this journey with you and can't wait for all of our future endeavors. There's so much more to come.

FROM BETHANY

Justin, Jeremy, Jedidiah, and Josey—You're my heroes. Thanks for all the help with the housework, the hugs, the encouragement, and all the cups of coffee! You are my favorites.

Johnnie Alexander—Thanks for the million Face Times. Your support means everything, and I'm so glad we're on this writing journey together.

Jeffery Donley—Thanks for answering my questions on theology and being a listening ear when I needed one. I'm so proud of you. Go Bulls!

Jill Lancour—Thanks for dropping everything to come stay with the boys when Justin deployed the week before the book was due and letting me read sections out loud to you even when it was late at night. I couldn't have done this without you.

I also want to thank Victoria Duerstock, Deb Dutton, and Sarah Hart for the support, laughs, encouragement, and prayers. I love you guys!

To Michelle—My confidant, big sister, biz partner, and best friend. This has been a crazy ride and I wouldn't have done it with anyone else. I love you so much. I can't wait for us to make beef bourguignon and raspberry whatever à la *Julie & Julia*. I prayed for years for God to bring me my best friend, and I'm so glad it was you.

Notes

1. ALL-IN FAITH

1. Ralph F. Wilson, "#32. Touching the Hem of Jesus' Garment (Luke 8:40-48)," JesusWalk Bible Study Series, www.jesuswalk.com /lessons/8_40-48.htm.
2. "What Is the Significance of the Hem of Jesus' Garment?" End of the Matter website, October 16, 2015, http://endofthematter.com /2015/10/why-is-there-healing-in-the-hem-of-jesus-garment/.

2. YOU ARE USEFUL

1. "Platinum and Its Use," Total Materia website, www.totalmateria .com/page.aspx?ID=CheckArticle&site=ktn&NM=237.
2. "40 Years of Platinum Drugs for Cancer," Compound Interest website, www.compoundchem.com/2018/09/17/platinum-cancer/.
3. Rachel Ross, "Facts About Platinum," Live Science website, August 1, 2016, www.livescience.com/39144-platinum.html.
4. "40 Years of Platinum Drugs for Cancer," www.compoundchem.com /2018/09/17/platinum-cancer/.
5. Rick Warren, *The Purpose Driven Life: What on Earth Am I Here For?* (Grand Rapids: Zondervan, 2012), day 1.

3. YOU CAN WITHSTAND THE HEAT

1. "Durability of Platinum Plating," SPC Surface Treatment Experts, last modified January 22, 2019, www.sharrettsplating.com/blog /durability-platinum-plating/.

2. "The Bible Numerology Code Number 7," AstroVera, www.astro
vera.com/bible-religion/176-bible-number-7.html.

4. YOU ARE PRECIOUS

1. Merriam-Webster, s.v. "precious metal," www.merriam-webster.com
/dictionary/precious%20metal.
2. Andrew Hecht, "Platinum Versus Gold: Both Precious Metals but
Which Is More Precious?" The Balance, last modified April 25,
2018, www.thebalance.com/platinum-versus-gold-808974.
3. "How Rare Is Platinum?" APMEX website, www.apmex.com
/education/bullion/how-rare-is-platinum.
4. "$52m for the World's Most Expensive Car—Why Does the Ferrari
250 GTO Cost So Much?" Arnold Clark Newsroom, last modified
October 9, 2013, www.arnoldclark.com/newsroom/334-52m-for
-the-world-s-most-expensive-car-why-does-the-ferrari-250-gto-cost
-so-much.
5. Emma Fierberg, "Why Louboutin Shoes Are So Expensive," Business Insider, last modified October 3, 2018, www.businessinsider
.com/why-christian-louboutin-shoes-are-so-expensive-red-bottoms
-heels-2018-9.
6. C. Isaiah Smalls II, "These Are the Most Expensive Game-worn
Basketball Shoes Ever Auctioned," The Undefeated, last modified
December 6, 2017, https://theundefeated.com/features/the-most
-expensive-game-worn-basketball-shoes-ever-auctioned-nike
-michael-jordan/.
7. "Kent & Vyxsin," The Amazing Race Wiki, https://amazingrace
.fandom.com/wiki/Kent_%26_Vyxsin.

5. YOU ARE RARE

1. Predating Ben Parker's quote from *Spider-Man* are several others,
including a verse in Luke 12:48. Check out this article with all the
details: Darryl Seland, "With Great Power Comes Great Responsibility," Quality Magazine, April 16, 2018, www.qualitymag.com
/articles/94643-with-great-power-comes-great-responsibility.
2. "The Mysterious White Metal That's Rarer Than Gold," Platinum
Jewelry.com, https://platinumjewelry.com/why-platinum/rare/.

3. "Mysterious White Metal," https://platinumjewelry.com/why -platinum/rare/.

4. Donald McDonald, "The Platinum of New Granada," Johnson Matthey Technology Review, accessed April 3, 2019, www.technology .matthey.com/article/4/1/27-31/.

5. Paul Tassi, "Why Isn't 'Fortnite' Going Away?" Forbes.com, January 4, 2019, www.forbes.com/sites/insertcoin/2019/01/04/why-isnt -fortnite-going-away/#11f3f6d64380.

6. "Here's the Psychology Behind Why We Like Expensive Things," Business Insider, www.businessinsider.com/sc/why-we-like -expensive-things-2018-12.

7. Emma Hargadon, "What Actually Makes This Bag Worth £162,500?" Who What Wear, www.whowhatwear.com/birkin -bag-prices/slide6.

8. Eva Marie Everson, "Ruth: Gleaning in the Fields of Jesus," Cross walk.com, www.crosswalk.com/faith/spiritual-life/ruth-gleaning-in -the-the-fields-of-jesus-1166975.html.

6. Your Faith Shines Brightly

1. "About Caregiving," National Care Planning Council, www.long termcarelink.net/eldercare/caregiving.htm.

7. You Were Created to Bond

1. J. Yeo, "Does Elohim foreshadow the Trinity in Genesis 1?" Theological Matters, April 10, 2018, https://theologicalmatters.com/2018 /04/10/does-elohim-foreshadow-the-trinity-in-genesis-1/.

2. Megan Senger, "Lessons from the School of Sales," *IDEA Fitness Journal*, June 30, 2011, www.ideafit.com/fitness-library/lessons-from -the-school-of-sales.

3. Lee Davenport, "Home Sales Success and Personality Types: Is There a Connection?" *Journal of Real Estate Practice and Education* vol. 21, no. 1 (2018): 29–57.

4. Dallas Willard, *Hearing God: Developing a Conversational Relationship with God* (Downer's Grove, IL: InterVarsity, 2012), 12.

8. You Are Malleable in the Father's Hands

1. Rachel Ross, "Facts About Platinum," Live Science, last modified August 1, 2016, www.livescience.com/39144-platinum.html.

9. You Can Resist Corrosion

1. John H. Walton, *Genesis*, The NIV Application Commentary (Grand Rapids, MI: Zondervan, 2011).
2. "Platinum," Corrosion Source, www.corrosionsource.com/Periodic Table/Platinum.

10. You Can Replace Your Heavy Heart with God's Heavy Presence

1. Barry Lenson, "Hunting for Platinum? These Three Facts Can Help You Find More," Specialty Metals, last modified March 8, 2017, www.specialtymetals.com/blog/2017/3/8/hunting-for-platinum -these-three-facts-can-help-you-find-more.
2. "The Manifestations of the Spirit in the Scripture," People Get Ready, last modified March 31, 2019, http://peoplegetready.org /holy-spirit/manifestations-spirit-scripture/.
3. David Jaffe, "Kavod—Dignity," Rabbi David Jaffe website, https:// rabbidavidjaffe.com/kavod-dignity/.

11. You Are Special

1. Dictionary.com, s.v. "commodity," www.dictionary.com/browse /commodity.
2. John H. Walton, *Genesis*, The NIV Application Commentary (Grand Rapids: Zondervan, 2011), 586.

12. You Can Be Self-Controlled

1. "Metals Science Lesson," Home Science Tools, https://learning -center.homesciencetools.com/article/metals-101/.
2. Terence Bell, "Platinum Group Metals (PGMs)," The Balance, www .thebalance.com/platinum-group-metals-pgms-2340166.

3. Michaeleen Doucleff and Jane Greenhalgh, "How Inuit Parents Teach Kids to Control Their Anger," National Public Radio, www .npr.org/sections/goatsandsoda/2019/03/13/685533353/a-playful -way-to-teach-kids-to-control-their-anger.

4. Darris McNeely, "Lessons from the Parables: Why Christ Spoke in Parables," UCG.org, www.ucg.org/the-good-news/lessons-from-the -parables-why-christ-spoke-in-parables.

13. You Are Authentic

1. Dictionary.com, s.v. "authentic," accessed May 25, 2019, www .dictionary.com/browse/authentic.

2. Barry Lenson, "How to Tell the Difference Between Silver, White Gold and Platinum," Specialty Metals, last modified April 1, 2015, www.specialtymetals.com/blog/2015/3/31/how-to-tell-the -difference-between-silver-white-gold-and-platinum.

3. Abigail Abrams, "Yes, Imposter Syndrome Is Real. Here's How to Deal with It," *Time* magazine, http://time.com/5312483/how-to -deal-with-impostor-syndrome/.

4. Abrams, "Yes, Imposter Syndrome Is Real."

14. Rainbow Kisses and Silver-Dime Hugs

1. "Judges 6:37," Bible Hub, https://biblehub.com/commentaries /judges/6-37.htm.

2. "What Does a Rainbow Mean in the Bible?" Bible Study, www.bible study.org/question/what-does-a-rainbow-symbolize-in-bible.html.

About the Authors

Business partners, coauthors, and besties **Michelle Medlock Adams** and **Bethany Jett** share enthusiasm for helping women, equipping other writers, and encouraging everyone they encounter. Because of their shared passions, this dynamic duo collaborates on many projects, including their first two books together releasing in 2019, *They Call Me Mom* and *Platinum Faith*. Owners of Platinum Literary Services, a premier literary firm, Adams serves as president and Jett serves as vice president. Both specialize in ghostwriting, developmental editing, nonfiction and children's books, and book proposals, as well as marketing strategies and best practices in social media. Both Adams and Jett are popular teachers on the writers' conference circuit, literary agent scouts for Cyle Young Literary Elite agency, and much-sought-after speakers at women's events and retreats.

Michelle Medlock Adams is an inspirational speaker, award-winning journalist, and best-selling author, earning top honors from the Associated Press, the Society of Professional Journalists, and the Hoosier State Press Association. In fact, she has garnered more than forty industry awards for her articles and books, including several Illumination gold medals, numerous Selah awards, the Advanced Writers and Speakers Association's prestigious Golden Scroll award, and the Selah's Book of the Year for her children's book *God Knows You*. Author of more than ninety books with close to four million books sold, Adams is celebrating the recent release of her children's book *What Is America?* (WorthyKids/Hachette). Michelle is married to her high school sweetheart, Jeff, and they have two grown daughters, two sons-in-law, and three grandbabies. When not writing or teaching writing, she enjoys bass fishing with her hubby and cheering on the Chicago Cubs and all Indiana University sports teams.

Bethany Jett's motto is "Learn everything you can; teach as you go." She is a multiple award-winning author and ghostwriter and finds joy speaking across the country at conferences, retreats, and camps for writers, women, college students, and teens. An entrepreneur at heart, Jett co-owns Serious Writer, Inc, where she hosts an online writers academy and writers events across the country as well as internationally. Her passion for all things strategy-related combined with her love of social media led her to pursue her masters of fine arts in communication where she's studying marketing and public relations. Jett married her college sweetheart and became a military wife. She and her husband felt called into the youth ministry and served together for more than a decade before rejoining the military world. Jett is a home-schooling momma of boys, a suspense-novel junkie who describes herself as "mid-maintenance," and a lover of cute shoes and all things girly.

To learn more about Bethany and Michelle, visit their websites:

www.michellemedlockadams.com
www.bethanyjett.com
https://PlatLit.com